D1135487

04034303

WHAT ARE GARDENS FOR?

Rory Stuart

FRANCES LINCOLN LIMITED
PUBLISHERS

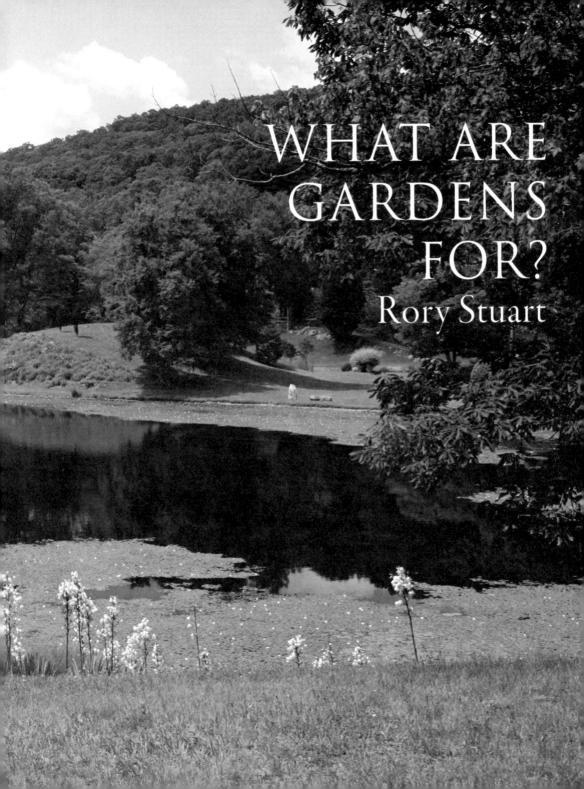

WHAT ARE GARDENS FOR?

Rory Stuart

Frances Lincoln Limited
www.franceslincoln.com

A catalogue record for this book is available from the British Library.

978-0-7112-3364-5

Printed and bound in China

1 2 3 4 5 6 7 8 9

Title page Innisfree, Millbrook, NY, USA

CONTENTS

'Such a garden as that of Lante is a world possession, and the builder of it like a great poet who has influenced the life of thousands, putting them in touch with the greatness of the past, lifting their thoughts and aspirations to a higher level, revealing to them the light of their own soul, opening their eyes to the beauty of the world.'

Sir George Sitwell, *On the Making of Gardens*

PREFACE

The subject of this book is the experience we have when we are in a garden. Its purpose is to help both the garden maker and the garden visitor to think harder about what gardens do to them, and can do for them – and thus to enjoy them more. If it seems full of repetitions and lacking in direction, that is because it circles this complex subject: thus in exploring how we can understand more fully the pleasures – physical, psychological and spiritual – that gardens give us I have often approached the same point from a different direction.

There are references to many other arts – music, literature, painting – because gardens, to be best understood, must be seen in the context of a culture. Gardeners and garden makers do not inhabit, and have never inhabited, a world of their own, cut off from contemporary developments in the other arts, fashion, politics and history. In some traditions, for example the Chinese, the totality of the nation's cultural history is of greater importance in making gardens than it is in the West, where a post-romantic emphasis on originality sometimes makes us forget our past, blurs our judgment and undermines the confidence of critics when faced with the very modern. In the conservative world of gardening this is, perhaps, less so than in the other arts, but it does happen.

Permission has been sought from the copyright holders of all the material quoted in this book, but if there are some chance omissions, these will be remedied in subsequent editions. I would like to thank the editors of the International Friends of Ninfa newsletter and of the *Garden Design Journal* for their permission to reuse material that first appeared in their publications. Thanks, too, to the owners of the Old Vicarage, East Ruston, for permission to use the aerial photograph of their garden. Thanks, again, to Anne Askwith, best of critical readers. And, as always, thanks to the many patient friends who have read parts of this work while it was in preparation, and whose suggestions have made it better than otherwise it would have been. Opinions expressed in this work remain, stubbornly, my own.

1 WHAT ARE GARDENS FOR?

'A garden is a real place imagined, and, with time and care, an imagined place made real.'

Patrick Lane

Dean Hole, the celebrated nineteenth-century rosarian, reported a wide variety of answers when he asked the question 'What are gardens for?'. 'Strawberries', a youngster replies. Those slightly older answer, 'tennis' and 'garden parties'. A horticultural bore opines, 'A garden is for botanical research and for the classification of plants.' A rapturous 'flapper' takes a different tack: 'What is a garden for? For the soul, sir, for the soul of the poet. For visions of the invisible, for grasping the intangible, for hearing the inaudible, for exaltations . . . above the miserable dullness of common life into the splendid regions of imagination and romance.' The first answers may be succinct to the point of being lapidary, and the last may be breathless gush, but all contain a grain of truth about the universal motives for garden making and for garden visiting. Among other things gardens are for food, fun and fantasizing. Remembering Jane Austen's heroines and all those significant walks in the shrubbery, we might extend the alliteration by adding 'flirtation'.

More seriously Professor David E. Cooper in his stimulating and modestly titled *A Philosophy of Gardens* suggests that gardens may also contribute to what he calls 'the good life'. He argues that many garden practices – that is what we do in gardens – 'induce virtues', and that gardens are '"hospitable" to various practices many of which . . . invite and attract certain virtues by providing especially appropriate opportunities for their exercise'. Many of us gardeners think that our gardens add to the quality of our lives, but are we really more virtuous because of our efforts combating the ground elder and pruning the roses? Fortunately Cooper goes on to specify the virtues he means. First, in looking after our plants we are exhibiting, he says, the virtue of care, 'a virtue that stands close to that of respect for life'. And by thus caring for our plants we enhance in ourselves a second virtue, self-discipline, a virtue that 'imposes a structure and pattern on a life that might otherwise be lacking in shape and unity'. Third, when the plant which has been the object of our tender care flowers or fruits, there is the delight in something to which we have contributed but which we could not have achieved alone, and this induces the virtue of humility. This close connection between humus and humility dates back at least to the monastic life of the Middle Ages. And this humility is related to a fourth virtue: that of patient hope, an optimistic expectation that things will turn out well, that the future has positive things to offer. Cooper does not cite the example but surely this is what Arthur Miller is getting at when he makes Willie Loman exclaim, towards the end of *Death of a Salesman*, 'Nothing's planted. I've nothing in the ground.' Willie feels himself cut off from any optimism about the future, so the play's audience can be little surprised that, shortly thereafter, he decides to kill himself.

Karel Čapek in *The Gardener's Year* light-heartedly supports what Cooper has to say about gardeners' behaviour. Here is Čapek on the care of plants during the darkest days of winter: 'If I knew it would help, I would wrap my holly in my own coat, and draw my pants over the juniper; I would take off my own shirt for you, Azalea pontica; I would cover you with my hat, Alum root, and for you, Coreopsis, nothing is left but my socks.' In a humorously exaggerated way he treats the plants like sentient beings – just as all gardeners do. Do we not all say of a plant, 'I don't think it's looking very happy today. I must do something for it'? Some of us even inquire of the plant, 'What's the matter with you?' Čapek also feels the humble sense of grace, of blessedness, when things go well and a plant comes into flower. He feels blessed because so much that made his plant bloom was not in his control, the weather in particular: 'With everything in the world it is possible to do something, but against weather nothing can be done. No zeal, no ambition, no newfangled methods, no meddling or cursing is of any use; the germ opens and a sprout comes up when it is time, and a law has been accomplished. Here you are humbly conscious of the impotence of man.' The virtuous behaviours of feeling humble and grateful, and of putting the needs of other living things above one's own, are all exemplified in Čapek's book.

Whether or not we feel more virtuous after working in a garden I am not sure, but certainly many of us feel healthier in body and mind after some garden work. It seems that this unselfish caring for our plants induces a mood that is healing, so that gardens provide opportunities both for caring for other lives and for curing ourselves. From my own experience I remember times when knotty problems have resolved themselves during a period of apparently mindless garden work – hand weeding, raking leaves or sawing logs. It is as though the job in hand requires just enough conscious attention to allow the unconscious mind to work out a solution to the gnawing problem, rather as in half-sleep a writer finds just the phrase for which his or her anxious, conscious mind had been searching all day; too often anxiety prevents the solution from becoming apparent. In discussing how a poem communicates with its reader, T.S. Eliot talked of a poem's meaning being like the drugged meat the burglar throws to the guard dog: the meaning occupies the conscious intellect while the poem 'goes to work' on the reader at a subtler level. Garden work has the same effect; monotonous activity in agreeable surroundings distracts the conscious mind, particularly when burdened with worry or tension, so that the unconscious mind can do its solving work.

Evidence, less anecdotal because it has been academically evaluated, of the healing power of garden work is provided by the charity Gardening Leave, set up by Anna Baker Cresswell in 2007 'to improve the mental and physical well-being of ex-Service personnel using Horticultural Therapy'. This brings together retired servicemen and women in a walled garden to learn and practise gardening skills, with the aim of helping them with their psychological and physical problems. The success of the project was evaluated in 2009 by Jacqueline Atkinson, Professor of Mental Health Policy at Glasgow University, who in her very positive report found that attendance at a Gardening Leave course was 'particularly helpful for veterans with post-traumatic stress disorder'. Atkinson interviewed many of the veterans, some of whom described their time working in the Gardening Leave garden as a 'life saver' – 'in the very real sense,' Atkinson goes on, 'of giving structure and a sense of achievement to those prone to serious bouts of depression'. She concludes her report, 'Gardening Leave is seen as having positive therapeutic benefits by the veterans who attend, and this was echoed by the clinical staff.'

It is not only those recovering from the traumas of war who can benefit from working in a garden. Andrew Barnett, a primary school head teacher, who had to give up work because of his bipolar disorder, also testifies to the healing power of gardening: 'I don't know what I would have done without this garden. [It] doesn't leave me time to feel sorry for myself – And it rewards me for my efforts with its fruits and its flowers' (quoted in the *Sunday Telegraph*, 10 October 2010). Again the feeling of being the recipient of some bounty is a strong element in his gratitude to the garden that in some senses has healed him. Diana Athill, a veteran but not of the military life, in her memoir *Somewhere Towards the End* writes of what gardening has given her: 'Getting one's hands into the earth, spreading roots, making a plant comfortable – it is a totally absorbing occupation, like painting or writing, so that you become what you are doing, and are given a wonderful release from consciousness of self.' This must be what the veterans working in Garden Leave's walled garden also find, as they leave behind their torments in caring for the plants. And this is why Athill, at the age of ninety-one, can write, 'However my bones may ache when I've done it [some garden work], I am always deeply refreshed by it.' Hard work that is refreshing – that is the miracle the garden offers.

One of the most moving testimonies to the healing power of a garden is that of Patrick Lane, the Canadian poet. In his memoir *What the Stones Remember: A Life Rediscovered* he tells of the year after he had finally abandoned the alcohol and drugs that had dominated his life for the previous forty-five years. He derives benefit not only from working in the garden but also from simply being in it and minutely observing its life. What the garden fosters are memories of his childhood, so that he can reconnect his present self with the pre-addiction boy he once was, thus making himself whole – in a psychological as well as a physical sense. (The connection between gardens and memory is something to which we shall return.) This is how he describes working in the garden: 'My hands are feeling again what they last felt when I was little more than a child. When I place my hands in the earth my fingers are like the tips of the first root of a seedling sprung to life. What I feel is wonder.' On another occasion, after he has been not working but simply meditating in the garden for an hour, he writes, 'The garden has started to heal my body.' The garden's peaceful, inexorable rhythms, its tranquil fixedness and the gardener's solitary concern for the life of other living things have begun to heal him both physically and mentally.

What is it about the garden experience that gives it this healing power? Working in the open air certainly makes sleeping easier, and the repetitive nature of some garden work has a calming effect. But the thing that many of us gardeners most appreciate in the garden is the lack of stress; time in gardens moves in relentless cycles whether we do our work or not. There will always be a chance next year to reseed the lawn, to move the azalea, to repair the path – to do tasks that this year we have neglected. Whatever kind of intervention we undertake, and whenever we intervene, we will have only a limited kind of influence. Things unfold in their own good time; we cannot hurry them even if we want to, any more than we can prolong the moment of heart-stopping beauty when a plant comes into flower. We must submit.

The garden reminds us that the rhythms of nature are different from those of human life, with its inexorable movement towards age and death – those of nature appear to be cyclical, while the rhythms of human life are all too clearly linear. Jacques in Shakespeare's *As You Like It* sums up the progress of human life in his cynical way, using a vegetable metaphor: 'From hour to hour we ripe and ripe,/And then from hour to hour we rot and rot.' The distinction between the two different kinds of time is more beautifully caught by Philip Larkin in his poem 'The Trees':

> The trees are coming into leaf
> Like something almost being said;
> The recent buds relax and spread,
> Their greenness is a kind of grief.
>
> Is it that they are born again
> And we grow old? No, they die too.
> Their yearly trick of looking new
> Is written down in rings of grain.
>
> Yet still the unresting castles thresh
> In fullgrown thickness every May.
> Last year is dead, they seem to say,
> Begin afresh, afresh, afresh.

This constant renewal adds an optimistic buoyancy to a gardener's spirits; it is only apparent, of course, because shrubs, flowers and trees also age and die. In the garden we are put in touch with eternal, seasonal rhythms that ignore us. The Persian poet Omar Khayyám, contemplating his own death and the world without him, wrote in great humility: 'Alas, without me for a thousand years/The rose will blossom and the spring will bloom.' Nature gets on with its work; we can make some small temporary interventions, but gardens are the most fragile of works of art, and if our care is suspended the ash trees and the ground elder, the nettles and the couch grass, will resume their sway.

In the late seventeenth century Sir William Temple understood some of the pleasures humans derive from gardening, as he wrote in his influential 'Upon the Gardens of Epicurus': 'The sweetness of the air, the pleasantness of smells, the verdure of plants, the cleanness and lightness of food, the exercise of working or walking; but above all, the exemption from cares and solicitude, seem equally to favour and improve both contemplation and health, the enjoyment of sense and imagination, and thereby the quiet and ease of the body and the mind.'

Most gardeners, of course, are not recovering drug abusers, or sufferers from post-traumatic stress disorder, or bipolar. But the kind of psychological re-balancing both gardeners and, sometimes, garden visitors find in gardens and gardening shares much with the healing experienced by these sufferers. A letter has just arrived on my desk telling of the calming, consoling effect a garden – not her own – had had on a friend who had recently lost her father. As Frederic Eden wrote when describing the creation of his garden in Venice (it came to be called, inevitably, the Garden of Eden), 'There is no pursuit, as has been found by big men and small, that will so readily and healthily take a man out of himself and away from his pain and grief, physical and moral.' We gardeners feel the tranquillity of being among living things that do not move and make little noise, that obey a cyclical rhythm that is not our own, and over which we have limited influence. In handling living things tenderly we enjoy atavistic, tactile pleasures while expressing care for the developing plants. Whether we are feeling the need to release some energy or just to sit and meditate, whether we feel sociable or in need of solitude – whatever our physical and psychological needs at any particular moment, with their different kind of temporal rhythms gardens can offer us what we are looking for.

ooooo

Gardens are also places where we can express ourselves as artists, in the process defining our own personalities. Medieval Scottish poets were known as 'makars', makers, and the very word 'poet' comes from the Greek verb meaning 'to make'; in making gardens we become artists, creators, or, to put it more precisely, place makers, which is the term the great landscaper Lancelot 'Capability' Brown always used when referring to himself. The gardens we make are 'places', not

Frederic Eden's garden in Venice, 1903

spaces, because they have been deliberately made, including certain plants and objects, excluding others; and because of this deliberate selection they are endowed with significance. This may be another reason why they have healing qualities. Unlike a space, a place is organized, sometimes around a central lawn, tree or pool, and it has limits; the walled gardens where the recovering servicemen and women of Gardening Leave work are obviously, and importantly, enclosed and thus safe. One of the reasons that children love gardens is that they can often find in them a place to make their own – a den, a secret corner, away from the world controlled by adults.

Man began to organize inchoate space when he built fences around areas of special importance; the word 'garden' comes from a root that identifies a place fenced off – from marauding animals, thieves and enemies. In the ancient world, even without a fence a wild space could be made a sacred place by building a temple, shrine or altar, often near a spring of water, so that the space seemed to organize itself around that structure. Seneca in one of his letters talks of how people would 'erect altars where great streams burst out from hidden sources'; the life-giving stream was a gift to the humans who depended on it, and to ensure the continued flow of water the powers of the underworld had to be thanked and placated in the temple. Petrarch recalled these words of Seneca when he came to make his own garden in the Vaucluse: 'Such altars . . . I have long thought of erecting, if opportunity should favour my wishes, there in my little garden.' There is often something almost sacred about the places we create, because in imposing themselves on the chaos of space humans were also discovering and expressing their own identity; to this day we continue to discover and reveal something of our identities in our gardens.

Rich and poor equally can be artists in the way they make their gardens. Gertrude Jekyll, with bracing Victorian common sense and directness, got to the heart of the matter: 'The size of a garden has very little to do with its merit. It is merely an accident relating to the circumstances of the owner. It is the size of his heart and brain and goodwill that will make his garden either delightful or dull, as the case may be, or raise it, in whatever degree he may, towards that of a work of fine art.'

Elizabeth von Arnim found her German garden a retreat: 'The garden is the place I go to for refuge and shelter, not the house. In the house are duties and annoyances, servants to exhort and admonish, furniture and meals; but out there blessings crowd round me at every step.' In the house she has an enforced role to play as the wife of a landowner, as the chatelaine running a large household, but in the garden she is free to be herself. She knows she has much to learn, but that does not prevent her expressing herself by arranging her flowers in 'clumps' (at much the same time Miss Jekyll, her older contemporary, was using the word 'drifts' to express a similar kind of more informal planting) rather than straight lines, however eccentric this seemed to her gardener. Elizabeth found a kind of freedom in her garden, freedom to express her individual personality, when in the house she had to fulfil a social role. Nelson Mandela found another kind of freedom in his prison garden on Robben Island: 'A garden was one of the few things in prison that one could control. To plant a seed, watch it grow, to tend it and then harvest it offered a simple but enduring satisfaction. The sense of being the custodian of this small patch of earth offered a small taste of freedom.' We are free in our gardens to do whatever is possible in that climate and soil; and what we choose to do will inevitably reveal something about our identities. Thus the visiting garden critic can 'read' the garden as evidence of the personality of its makers, and of the period and culture in which they lived.

Italian Renaissance gardens often contained inscriptions exhorting the visitor to enjoy the freedom that the garden bestowed, a freedom reminiscent, perhaps, of the mythical golden age of Arcadia, when careless shepherds and shepherdesses footed it fleetly upon the greensward. In the Villa Borghese gardens, for example, visitors would have read, 'Whoever you are, now be a free man, and fear not the fetters of the law'. So gardens have always been places where humans can feel freer than in the course of ordinary life, where we can plant what we like (which is not to say that it will grow), prune back what we choose, fill the space with colourful plants, or restrict ourselves to white flowers, or to green leaves and green grass. We can express ourselves both as creative and executive artists; we write the composition and perform it – that is if we are our own gardeners.

But can a garden be thought of as a work of art? The answer is: only to some extent. Works of art are human creations, or in the case of *objets trouvés* human selections and arrangements; but gardens are only in part the creations of the human will, as has been emphasized above. It was for this reason that Hegel denied that gardens could be classified as works of art. A second objection to calling gardens works of art is that they have no definite shape, since they lack a conclusion; instead, because they are dominated by time, they are in a constant state of evolution. But in so far as they are patterns of shape and colour organized in a controlled space by a human, they are, in part, works of art and thus capable of expressing meaning and personality. And in some ways it may be that the garden comes closer to what Wagner called the *Gesamkunstwerk,* the total artwork that involves all our senses, than those late nineteenth-century experiments with blending painting and music, such as Whistler's paintings entitled *Nocturnes*, or Debussy's Nocturnes, which the composer described as 'a study in grey painting'.

Some gardens express the personalities of their creators and their messages all too clearly. Louis XIV's Versailles in France with its *alleés* radiating from a single point and extending to the horizon's limits has an emphatic political message to convey – I am the Sun King and everything turns upon me. At the Villa d'Este in Italy Cardinal Ippolito used water as a plaything; nothing could have more plainly established the distance between his aristocratic self and the peasants of the Roman *campagna*, who worked the land (often his land) and for whom water was a vital resource, something much too important to be played with. In the twentieth century at San Simeon, on the coast of California, the press baron William Randolph Hearst wanted to show the world that he could have anything in his garden, as in his house, Hearst Castle, and so he had a bit of Spain, a bit of Italy and so on; the results are sadly ludicrous. The Vittoriale degli Italiani, the poet d'Annunzio's creation on the shores of Lake Garda in Italy, also communicates a strong sense of the creator's egotistical personality. In his garden we find the ships on which he performed so heroically and the aeroplane that he flew over Vienna; to complete this curious mixture of the military and the artistic there is a classical nymphaeum guarded by a field gun. The garden contains the components of the myth the poet and novelist created around himself; it shows us how he wanted to be seen – as man of action, lover and sensitive artist. And at the top of the highest point of the highest hill is the tomb of the fallen hero; this is the focus of the whole garden, the shrine at which the visitor is bidden to worship. Oh dear, yes, we reveal ourselves in our gardens.

The revelation of personality is only one of the meanings that the visitor can derive from a garden. We may also learn about the culture from which the garden maker came, about the period in which he or she lived; there may even be a story or a view of history implicit in the garden's layout, as at the Villa Lante in Italy (see Chapter 6). Sometimes meanings will be obvious only to someone from the same cultural background; this is particularly true of oriental gardens, where the expression of individual personality is the last thing we find. The fascination of the dry garden at Ryoan-ji in Japan derives from the fact that the fifteen stones are clearly deliberately placed, but why they are so placed and what the placing means is far from clear; we are challenged to think what the maker's purpose was in arranging the stones in just such a manner. This may explain this garden's continuing interest for so many people, from many different cultural backgrounds. At the other extreme some gardens' meanings are all too clear; they are driven home with blatant, literal force. This is particularly true of contemporary conceptualist gardens. Take the example of Nip Paysage's *Pause*, an installation in a busy public garden in Montreal. The creators tell us they wanted to say to the busy passers-by, 'It's OK to stop and sit down,' so they installed four giant chairs. Here beauty and proportion give way to the obvious message that is to be conveyed.

Martha Schwartz, the American designer, says she is 'guided by the desire to make landscapes that speak to people of the human condition', but I wonder if landscapes can speak; perhaps they communicate more successfully at a non-verbal level. The mention of Schwartz might remind us of another function that gardens sometimes, though not often, have: they make us laugh. She first came to public attention with her Bagel Garden, created in front of her Boston townhouse in 1979. In the small, rectangular space available she arranged two rows of carefully varnished bagels, set in purple aquarium gravel, between an outer box hedge and a box-edged bed planted with pink geraniums. Schwartz uses few plants and many bright colours in her work, and this has raised a storm of protest in some quarters. But she defends herself and the importance of humour vigorously: 'God help the person who thinks that humour is frivolous. I think the fire and brimstone preachers get listened to a lot less than the comedians.'

We have identified many answers to Dean Hole's question 'What are gardens for?' – giving care, being healed, self-expression, communication, humour. Many gardeners today also want to grow their own food, so that it can be eaten fresh and be guaranteed free from chemicals. Gardens are places apart – apart, for example, from the world of supermarket fruit, standard in size, shape and colour; apart from the world of tidied, sprayed verges so inimical to wild flowers and butterflies. But we have not yet touched on the thing that most people want from their gardens: beauty. Mara Miller, in her book *The Garden as an Art*, writes, 'In America . . . the expectations people bring to gardens and the pleasures they find there are overwhelmingly aesthetic.' If people are ambitious to make a beautiful garden, they may read some of the many books telling them about how plant colours should be placed side by side, how to create a successful herbaceous border, even how to design their garden. What these books are really doing is passing on the contemporary view on what constitutes good taste (see Chapter 5), but fashions change and with them the view of what is tasteful, even of what is beautiful. Sir Kenneth Clark, the art historian, points out that the amount of time one can spend responding to beauty is limited: 'I fancy that one cannot enjoy a pure aesthetic sensation (so called) for longer than one can enjoy the smell of an orange, which in my case is less than two minutes.' Gardens must have more to offer than beauty, if they are to continue contributing so much to our lives.

ooooo

The attentive reader may by now have noticed that I have been dancing round a difficult question – difficult to express without lurching into fey, quasi-religious language, and certainly difficult to answer. The question is this: to what extent do gardens offer us spiritual (the word should be understood in a pre-religious or an a-religious way) as well as psychological and physical rewards? In his book *The Idea of the Holy* (translated by John W. Harvey) Rudolf Otto describes some of the feelings that occur when we experience the holy: 'The feeling of it [what he calls the *mysterium tremendum*] may come sweeping like a gentle tide, pervading the mind with a tranquil mood of deepest worship. It may pass over into a more set and lasting attitude of the soul, continuing, as it were, thrillingly vibrant and resonant until at last it dies away and the soul resumes its "profane", non-religious mood of everyday experience.' Or the sense of the holy 'may burst with sudden eruption up from the depths of the soul with spasms and convulsions, or lead to the strangest excitements'. Or, again, 'it may become the hushed, trembling, and speechless humility of the creature in the presence of – whom or what? In the presence of that which is a *mystery* inexpressible and above all creatures'. We can all recognize these different feelings from our experience of music, and perhaps of some of the visual arts; gardens, too, stimulate these contradictory feelings of excitement and peace.

Addison, a self-confessed deist, spoke of how 'A beautiful prospect delights the soul', and he goes on to show that it is not only the beauty of the prospect that delights but the fact that it is composed largely of natural things. He cites 'huge Heaps of Mountains, high Rocks and Precipices', 'Groves, Fields and Meadows', 'Rivers, Jetteaus and falls of Water' (these 'Jettaus' are fountains, and therefore the only man-made item in his catalogue). The point he is making is that a beautiful landscape or garden does not delight our souls in the same way as a beautiful poem, painting or symphony. A composition of natural things seems to communicate something more spiritually uplifting, or uplifting in a different way. Is that just because of the scale of the components, or is there something else?

I suspect the answer lies buried deep in our psyches, at some primitive level that will be hard to excavate. In most primitive religions great trees, significant rocks and important wells were worshipped; these objects remained sacred in the folk memory long after the advent of Christianity, or any other of the monotheistic religions. Shinto, with its belief in the *kami* or spirits that inhabit rocks, waterfalls and trees, still informs many of the traditions of garden making in Japan. The Japanese have thus preserved a reverence for the individual objects

In the Japanese garden each component of the composition is given careful attention

that make up their and our gardens – something that has been lost in the West. The historian Tom Holland has an interesting view on this: 'Once, before the Church had begun its great labour of erecting a boundary between the sacred and the profane, the two had seemed interfused. Streams and trees had been celebrated as holy; laymen had laid claim to visions; prophets had read the future in ox dung; mourners had brought offerings of food and drink to tombs. Increasingly, however, the clergy had succeeded in identifying the dimensions of the supernatural as exclusively their own. By the eighth century, Christians uninitiated into the priesthood were losing confidence in their ability to communicate with the invisible,' he writes. If in the eighth century the lay person was losing contact with the world of the supernatural, how much more difficult is it for us to understand anything of this supra-mundane world and our response to it, when science has laid bare so many of what were its mysteries.

Children are often particularly sensitive to what we might clumsily call the spiritual emanations of nature, perhaps because they are uninstructed in science. Wordsworth, in a famous passage from *The Prelude*, recalls the time when a mountain seemed to rise up and admonish his young self for stealing a boat. Much more recently in the Italian gardening magazine *Gardenia* Gian Lupo Osti, the celebrated peony breeder and dendrologist, recalls a childhood time when, like Wordsworth, he escaped from his parents (who were devoted to their post-prandial snooze): 'I would go for a walk (preferably alone) in a wood dense with tall trees, and halt before a single ancient tree; there I would undergo an experience I would call spiritual, today I might even call it religious.' Were these children responding in their primitive way to something in nature that we adults also respond to, but subliminally, and often without being able to articulate such deeply buried feelings? Certainly remarkable trees have long been worshipped, such as yew trees, like the one at Tandridge in Surrey that predates the earliest church on the site, and is believed to have been considered holy. Thomas Packenham, an adult with a self-confessed addiction to trees, still experiences something of this spiritual magic; he writes, 'To visit these trees, to step beneath their domes and vaults, is to pay homage at a mysterious shrine.'

The practice of celebrating a water source by decorating it with flowers and pictures, 'well-dressing' as it is called, many think dates back to Celtic times. Christians were opposed to this ancient, pagan custom and in sixteenth-century England Thomas Cromwell ordered all well-dressing equipment to be destroyed. This even though in the Middle Ages the sacred wells had been rededicated to Christian saints, so that today we have in England, among many others, St Winifred's Well in Holywell, St Chad's Well in Lichfield and St Keyne's in Cornwall. The religion may change but the places that are sacred remain the same, and they are marked by natural objects that are often components of our gardens – water, rocks and trees.

Mountains are sacred in many faiths – Ayer's Rock in Australia, Mount Kailas in Tibet and Mount Fuji in Japan are just three examples. Stones, too, are often considered to have special spiritual significance, sometimes indeed special powers. Standing stones at Stonehenge or the Rollright stones in Oxfordshire mark places felt to be of inexplicable, and therefore magical, power. One of the most sacred of stones in the world is the black stone in one corner of the Ka'aba at Mecca. This almost certainly had religious significance in pre-Islamic times; that the prophet Mohammed kissed it suggests it was already recognized as a source of spiritual power. The Japanese have an acute perception of the spiritual power of rocks, an important component of all oriental gardens. In the eleventh century *Sakuteiki* the Japanese garden maker is advised to 'Choose a particularly splendid stone and set it as the main stone. Then, following the request of the first stone, set others accordingly.' If the garden maker ignores the advice of the stone and sets the other stones incorrectly, then disaster will over take the household, particularly if the incorrectly placed stone becomes an *ishigami*, that is a demon stone. Contemporary Japanese designers still talk of listening to what the stones say.

Is this attention to the supernatural power of water and trees, stones and mountains just primitive religion (another word for this might be 'magic') or an appeal to some primeval, Jungian level of the universal subconscious? I am not sure, but natural objects, whether in a garden or a landscape, sometimes have a powerful spiritual effect on humans, even if we are unable to express in words precisely what that effect is. When it comes to spiritual sensitivity, we are the victims of our scientific age and of the monotheistic religions with their emphasis on guilt, obligation and the afterlife. In our sophistication we have, perhaps, forgotten how to communicate with the world that surrounds us and to experience it directly in all its complexity. But, maybe, in making gardens we are creating places where such feelings can be enjoyed, though such creations may never have quite the spiritual force of objects found in nature, like Gian Lupo Osti's tree or Wordsworth's mountain.

Curiously, flowers seem never to have had quite the same spiritual potency as rocks, water and trees. They were not the object of a religious cult, though they were used in magic spells to ward off sickness, accidents and the evil eye, and their symbolism was important in Christian painting – the lily representing purity, the rose the symbol of the Virgin Mary and so on. When the tulip was celebrated in the palace of Topkapi, and tortoises with candles stuck on their backs wandered through the tulip beds, this was a purely secular festivity, an occasion for wine and dancing girls. In the English tradition flowers are seldom seen as individual objects. Exceptions to this are the flowers presented for competition at flower shows; individual blooms are then subject to the intense scrutiny of a judging panel. There was also a time when auriculas were shown in theatres with a black velvet backcloth and sometimes with a mirror placed behind them, so that the beauties of the individual plant could be appreciated in 360 degrees. In paintings flowers are also given individual attention, but for their aesthetic or botanical interest, not their spiritual value. The English flower garden is a distinctly secular invention, where nature is firmly controlled and colourful flowers displayed in herbaceous or mixed borders become paints on an artist's palette, displaying the taste and flair of the artist, not the wonder of the flower itself. And it should not be forgotten that flowers can detract from the atmosphere of a place, a point demonstrated again and again in romantic Italian ruins where the visitor's experience is marred by distracting flower beds pockmarked with pink begonias. In many an English flower garden we are very far from an appreciation of the divine spirit immanent in a fine rock, an ancient tree, a dark pool or any other single, natural object; the flowers are a distraction, and often inhibit any spiritual experience the visitor may have.

In an interesting essay entitled 'The Garden as Metaphor' Clare Cooper Marcus discusses the ideal lands that were the inventions of early civilizations; for the Greeks such a land was the country of the Hyperboreans, where death and old age were unknown; for early Tibetan Buddhists it was Shambhala, a place where peace and wisdom ruled. Such perfect countries cannot survive the prying satellite eye of Google Earth, but perhaps a desire to find such an ideal land, even if only in our imaginations, is one motive that drives us to make our own ideal places. Marcus goes on to argue that one of the satisfactions in garden making is that 'it enables [gardeners] to marry two modes of thought – intuitive/ logical, right brain/left brain, feminine/masculine – and by so doing, to resolve certain inner conflicts that remain in the individual and the group psyche.' We garden because that activity requires knowledge and intuition, science and nurturance[?], planning and faith.' Perhaps one of our motives for garden making is that it puts us in touch with a more primitive level of our beings, with an instinctive pantheism, which allows us, for example, to reverence the largest living things human beings encounter – trees – and the sources of our life – light and water.

ooooo

We have moved far from the point where many gardeners begin – when the garden is just the piece of land left over after the house has been built. At such a point we may want to fill the space as fast as possible, or, if we live in the US, to get in our foundation plants, which aim to give the house a more settled and permanent look. But once we have taken these initial steps, we may begin to raise the fundamental question that is the subject of this book, and then we shall begin to ask a lot more both of the garden we are making and of the gardens that we visit.

2 GARDEN VISITING

'You open the gate to a garden as you would open the first page of a new book, with the hope of living a moment of happiness in the discovery of a place, a story, a human adventure, a time to dream, away from the bustle of everyday life, dream and escape . . . a moment outside of time.'

Quoted in Louisa Jones, *The Garden Visitor's Companion*

Do we visit gardens belonging to strangers or friends for some of the same reasons that we make gardens? Many non-gardening visitors are in search of some kind of beauty, particularly the tranquil and fragile beauty that a garden especially offers. Gardens, initially private but later also public, have always been places of escape, and are even more so in the twenty-first century – escape from a world where things change too fast and unpredictably, where there is too much noise, too much dirt, too much aggression. This escape appeals particularly to the ageing, when they begin to feel increasingly at odds with the world they live in; and this is one reason why so many begin gardening after the age of fifty. By that age also our children are grown and we need a new focus for our caring; and maybe by then we have learned patience.

If we live in an urban flat, a garden or park allows us the pleasure of walking in the open air, perhaps on soft grass rather than unyielding pavements. Then we may also want to visit a nearby private garden because we are curious; we want to know what the neighbours are doing, and what they are like. Perhaps we will take an opportunity of an open-garden day to peak behind their curtains, or ask to use the lavatory to get a glimpse of the house. We want to know what kind of people they are, and their garden will tell us something of that. Another reason for visiting a garden is that we may just want a day out, away from an irksome routine, so that the garden is merely an excuse for a journey. In recent years the media have emphasized that gardens are part of the world of fashion, so, finally, we may visit a garden to see what the latest 'in' thing is; have concrete, plastic and steel finally ousted the plants?

If we are gardeners, we may visit other gardens to get ideas on how to improve the layout of our own garden; we may also want to see what plants will grow in the locality, plants we had never previously thought possible for us. We may want to learn, and so will arrive, notebook in hand, ready to write down the names of plants new to us, which otherwise we will never remember. Perhaps we will also write down a design idea derived from the siting of a bench, the handling of water or the style of a path edging. We will want to compare our garden with the one being visited, to see what its owners do better, perhaps in their plant and colour combinations, and what (more consolingly) they do worse, perhaps ditto. As the American designer Joe Eck writes: 'The more one looks at gardens, actually or in books, and the more one thinks about them and tries to isolate what is pleasing about them (or not), the better one's own garden is likely to be. Like any other art, gardening begins with borrowing.' And gardeners especially appreciate the fact that all this pleasure can be enjoyed without having to stir a finger. In our own gardens relaxation is too often interrupted by the thought of tasks neglected, or the sight of a draggle-headed dahlia that needs instant staking.

In order to get more out of the experience, we must learn to improve our garden visiting. First, we must experience the garden being visited with no less intensity and completeness than we would an opera, a novel or a piece of sculpture. T.S. Eliot in a letter to Stephen Spender says this about reading a poem and then writing critically about it: 'You have to give yourself up, and then recover yourself, and the third moment is having something to say, before you have wholly forgotten both surrender and recovery.' In such a complex, sensuous work of art as a garden our senses may be overwhelmed in the process of 'giving ourselves up'; there are so many smells, sights and sounds. Addison thought the eye the most important sense in the garden, but was delighted to welcome birds: 'I value my garden more for being full of blackbirds than cherries, and very frankly give them fruit for their songs', he wrote (and some people called his age 'the Age of Reason'!). Smells can be the most distracting part of our experience, since nothing is so powerful in triggering memory, though they are almost impossible to remember; the merest waft of a smell can transport us back to a half-forgotten place perhaps thousands of miles distant, while the rational brain is powerless to intervene. The mysterious way that smells work is well caught by Proust (translated by Scott Moncrieff and Kilmartin): the young boy is standing in front of the hawthorns he admires so much, 'breathing in their invisible and unchanging odour, trying to fix it in my mind (which didn't know what to do with it)'.

Even the eye, at whose delight most gardens are aimed, can be educated. Robin Lane Fox, one of the best writers on gardens as well as on plants, comments that too often, when visiting gardens, 'we concentrate our eyes and attention on flowers. It is an understandable prejudice, but with a little training and a little more attention it is easy to start noticing where before one had only been seeing and thus to pick out details of form, outline, and reflection which the dedicated searcher for flowers would normally hurry past.' The eye delights in colour, but, as Lane Fox points out, it misses much if it sees nothing more, viewing the garden as a collection of plants or a series of pictures, and failing to appreciate the sculptural qualities of the plantings, and the architectural qualities of the garden's design.

Then there are the intangible, non-sensory elements in garden appreciation – what we can only call the atmosphere of the place. This will depend to a large extent on the visitor's sensitivity, experience, imagination and reading, but it will also be the product of the garden's design, and this may well reveal a part of its story, particularly if we are visiting a historic garden. Thus at the Bagh-e Fin in Kashan, Iran, the fact that an eminent politician was murdered in the bath house that lies on one side of the garden may cast a sinister light over our whole experience of the garden, so that, for all the gaiety of the fountains, falls and water rills, its symmetrical perfection seems coldly threatening. Here, of course, it is the visitor's imagination that affects the impact of the garden, but many gardens have a peculiarly potent effect on the imagination, and we would be wrong to ignore its promptings.

John D. Sedding has written very well on the appeal of old gardens to our memory and imagination.

> In the case of old gardens, mellowed by time, we have, I say,
> to note something that goes beyond mere surface beauty. Here
> we may expect to find a certain superadded quality of pensive
> interest, which, in so far as it can be reduced to words, tells of the
> blent influences of past and present, of things seen and unseen,
> of the joint effects of Nature and Man. The old ground embodies
> the bygone conceptions of ideal beauty; it has absorbed human
> thoughts and memories; it registers the bequests of time. Dead

Bagh-e-Fin, Kashan, Iran

men's traits are exemplified here. The dead hand still holds sway. The pictures it conjured still endure, its cunning is not forgotten, its strokes still make the garden's magic, in shapes and hues that are unchanged save for the slow moulding of the centuries. *Really*, not less than metaphorically, the garden growths do keep green the memories of the men and women who placed them there, as the flower that is dead still holds its perfume.

And our reading may help the imagination to work. William Beckford, visiting the Belvedere of the Vatican palace, and perhaps beginning to feel the pangs of hunger, paused to enjoy the evening light at a spot which 'brought the scenery of an antique Roman garden full into my mind. I expected every instant to be called to the table of Lucullus hard by, in one of the porticoes, and to stretch myself on his purple triclinia.' The invitation never came, but Beckford turned home 'delighted with a ramble that had led my imagination so far into antiquity'.

Literature and its associations may also encourage us to see a garden differently. Who could visit the garden of Lamb House at Rye in Sussex without imagining Henry James in tightly buttoned waistcoat giving instructions to the gardener? In the same garden, and even more irresistible perhaps, will be memories of E.F. Benson's Miss Mapp and Lucia, the former doing her aerobics in her *giardino segreto* while being spied upon from the church tower by the latter. James's fictional gardens are always of great significance, particularly as symbols of the deep-rooted, shadowiness (often moral shadowiness) of Europe in comparison to brash, brightly lit, sometimes innocent America. The teatime scene under the cedar tree at the beginning of *The Portrait of a Lady* is characteristic of James, a writer who had transplanted himself from America to England. In this passage from his *The Princess Casamassima* the garden visitor is Hyacinth Robinson, would-be revolutionary and assassin, responding in a way we might not expect to the atmosphere of an ancient, aristocratic garden:

> He rambled an hour in breathless ecstasy, brushing the dew from the deep fern and bracken and the rich borders of the garden, tasting the fragrant air and stopping everywhere, in murmuring rapture, at the touch of some exquisite impression . . . He had been dreaming all his life of just such a place . . . There was something in the way the grey walls rose from the green lawn that brought

tears to his eyes; the spectacle of long duration un-associated with some sordid infirmity or poverty was new to him; he had lived with people among whom old age meant for the most part a grudged and degraded survival. In the favoured resistance of Medley was a serenity of success, and an accumulation of dignity and honour.

James himself had found something of the same atmosphere in Oxford college gardens; he wrote of them: 'They struck us as the fairest things in England and the ripest and sweetest fruit of the English system. Locked in their antique verdure, guarded, as in the case of New College, by gentle battlements of silver-grey outshouldering the matted leafage of undisseverable plants, filled with nightingales and memories, a sort of chorus of tradition.' The wonderfully chosen words 'outshouldering' and 'undisseverable' convey something of the sensuous quality James responded to in these ancient gardens. Above all readers, who have been familiar in their youth with *The Secret Garden* or with *Alice in Wonderland*, will never be able to push open the door in a garden wall without a sense of excitement.

James reminds us also of how gardens often prompt memories, and memories may also affect the way we make gardens. To speak of my own garden experience, I have planted a 'Mermaid' rose in every garden I have made. At least in part this must be because I remember the 'Mermaid' rose growing up the front of my grandmother's house in Hampshire. It was the first plant I ever noticed, ever learned to name. Gardens of childhood are particularly potent in the human imagination; perhaps because those who enjoy happy childhoods are all driven out of their Gardens of Eden by maturity.

Some gardens set out to assault the visitor's imagination, occasionally too blatantly. At Hawkstone Park in Shropshire the terrifying narrow defiles through the rock, the insubstantial rope bridge, and, above all, the hermit with his goat's beard, aimed to transport the thrilled eighteenth-century visitor into a world that was excitingly primitive. Francis Dashwood's park at West Wycombe in Buckinghamshire provided another kind of thrill, the shock of the pagan – hellfire caverns, a reproduction of the river Styx and a cursing well. His Temple of Venus was peopled by carved satyrs and monkeys, and further caves could be entered through an opening that was shaped like a vagina. Other gardens aim to stimulate both the visitor's mind and imagination rather than take it by storm. Ian Hamilton Finlay's Little Sparta near Edinburgh takes the traditional and reinterprets it; thus

Hawkstone Park, Shropshire,
England

the ornamental gates, which were usually crowned with stone pineapples, symbols
of fertility, are here topped with exploding hand grenades. We are forced to ask
'Why?', to think, What does this mean? Is our age more violent, less creative, more
destructive? Finlay also brought words into the garden to challenge (and sometimes
to tease) our intellects, so that a visit to his garden is not only a sensual experience.
One critic has described the concept of this garden as 'one of total experience',
meaning, perhaps, our senses are stimulated but also our brains.

Much influenced by Little Sparta is the contemporary work of art (it is hardly
appropriate to call it a garden) being made in Tuscany by the American sculptor
Sheppard Craige, Il Bosco della Ragnaia. In his sacred grove we can visit the
Centre of the Universe, the Altar of Skepticism (sic) inscribed with Montaigne's
words '*Que sais je?*', and, if we are puzzled by these experiences, we can consult
the Oracle of the Self. As in Finlay's gardens, carved words in the context
stimulate us into new, unexpected thoughts. Perhaps most important for the

Il Bosco della Ragnaia, San Giovanni d'Asso, Italy

garden critic seeking to immerse him or herself in the garden experience are the four plaques: 'Solo Qui', 'Solo Ora', 'Solo Così', 'Solo Questo' (Only Here, Only Now, Only Thus, Only This); good advice – concentrate on the moment and the present experience, immerse yourself in the 'now'; only when you have done this as completely as possible will you be able to judge the garden adequately. A visitor who follows this advice will never ask the garden owner the insulting question 'And when is this garden at its best?'

But for all this concentration on the moment and the visitor's determination to become immersed in the experience of the garden, memories of other gardens will also have an influence. The critic's memory will be full of gardens experienced in childhood or in literature and of others more recently visited, so that the garden we see before us will be seen through a lens already foggy with half-remembered details. The history of our native country and its culture will have an effect as well; stories from the Bible or the Koran will be buried in our memories, so we cannot make ourselves a kind of *tabula rasa*, ready to receive new impressions without being influenced by our personal and cultural pasts.

But let us step back a moment from this assault upon our senses, intellects and imaginations, reminding ourselves coolly that in visiting a garden we are looking at a work of art, but a work of art peculiarly complex since it is both natural and artificial, both temporary and permanent. And this work of art, most unusually, exists simultaneously in four dimensions; time, the fourth dimension, is a dominant influence in several ways – among others, in bringing plants to fruition and destruction, and then in changing the light even as one looks at the garden. The influence of time on the garden is seen in the changes that happen season by season, day by day, and in spring even hour by hour. We are constantly tempted to visit our own gardens to see what has changed, in spring perhaps even several times a day. Usually a work of art appeals to one sense at a time – painting and architecture to the eye, music to the ear, cooking to the palate and so on; it is only gardens which blur our reactions by stimulating so many senses simultaneously. In addition we cannot escape the consciousness of how fragile and temporary is the beauty we are admiring – which perhaps makes our enjoyment of that beauty especially poignant and sharp.

But in a garden, as in an art gallery, we do not only look for beauty in the works we see; perhaps we want to understand something of the artists' characters and attitudes, or something about the period they lived in. Or we may be looking for originality, an unexpected touch that will make us see all pictures and all places we visit freshly or differently. When we visit a Chinese garden and see a single twisted, ancient tree standing alone in a courtyard, or a single chrysanthemum in a pot, perhaps we will think how often in Western, particularly English, gardens we miss the beauty of a single flower or shrub by seeing it massed into a herbaceous or mixed border; the plant has taken its place in a colour scheme but at the expense of an appreciation of its complete, individual character. In gardens, as in art galleries and concert halls, our senses are delighted but we may also be stimulated to think.

ooooo

When we look, briefly, at the history of garden visiting we find plentiful evidence of all the motives that we have identified above – the search for new plants, and for the stimulus offered by an original work of art, the beauty and peace of a place that seems removed from the world, and so on. Avid plant hunters might have visited the Antwerp garden of Pieter van Coudeberghe, which some call the first botanical garden in Europe, in search of novel planting ideas. In 1567 Lodovico Guicciardi visited and wrote a description of the garden. Before the seventeenth century it was mainly the rich and diplomats from foreign countries who made visits to the gardens of strangers and their motive was curiosity. Thomas Platter of Basel, for example, describes a visit to the once-royal palace of Nonsuch in Surrey in 1599; he was more a tourist than a garden critic, praising the gardens as 'charming' and the topiary as 'very gay and attractive'. The most important visitor to the gardens of the nobility in this period was, of course, the Virgin Queen herself on one of her 'progresses'. She would expect regal entertainment, often a masque in the garden, and information about local attitudes to her government. These visits cost the hosts immense sums: when Elizabeth visited Dudley at Kenilworth in 1575, it is reckoned that her host spent £1,000 a day on her entertainment, perhaps £200,000 in today's money.

In the mid-seventeenth century young English gentlemen, keen to avoid the Civil War, set off to tour Italy, to learn that elegant blend of leisure and self-education that was summed up in the Latin phrase *otium cum dignitate*. Garden visiting stimulated their imaginations and gave them a particular 'frisson' of delight when they thought that the poets and historians of the Classical age might have trodden the same walks. John Evelyn, for example, visiting the Villa Aldobrandini in Frascati on 5 May 1645, was amazed at the beauty of the site and at the elaborate waterworks, concluding, 'I do not wonder that Cicero and others have celebrated this place with such encomiums,' though Cicero would not have seen the fountains and the orchestra of automata powered by water pressure that impressed Evelyn so much. In Paris, Evelyn also visited Pierre Morin's garden and copied the oval parterre he saw there in the garden he created at Sayes Court in Deptford. In the Garden of the World, as Italy was then often known, visitors looked at models they could copy in the development of their estates at home; an example is John Raymond, who in 1647 saw at the Villa d'Este in Tivoli 'my patterne for a Countrey seat'. The age of the 'florist' saw more exchanges of garden visits, though these were usually between friends or at least between victims of the same passion for collecting rare plants. And at the end of the century the indefatigable Celia Fiennes, travelling around England on horseback, found at Newcastle-on-Tyne that the Barber Surgeon's Hall had 'a pretty garden walled in, full of flowers, and greens in potts and in the borders'; she recorded what she saw but seldom passed judgment.

In early eighteenth-century England the sensuous delights of the pleasure gardens at Vauxhall were seen by some as a threat to Christian morality. Addison, as Mr Spectator, wrote: 'When I consider the fragrancy of the walks and bowers, with the choirs of birds that sung upon the trees, and the loose tribe of people that walked under their shades, I could not but look upon the place as a kind of Mahometan paradise.' Man first fell in a garden, and the sensuous delights on offer must have contributed to that event. One of the most popular private gardens to visit later in the century was The Leasowes in the West Midlands, the *ferme ornée* made by the poet William Shenstone, who was financially ruined by the scale of his ambition. Even the great literary critic, lexicographer and Shakespeare editor Samuel Johnson somewhat grudgingly acknowledged that when Shenstone began 'to point his prospects, to diversify his surface, to entangle his walks, and to wind his waters', he did so 'with such judgment and such fancy as made his little domain the envy of the great and the admiration of the skilful – a place to be visited by travellers and copied by designers'. Again garden visitors were looking for examples to copy in their own places, and The Leasowes had an enormous influence on the development of eighteenth-century taste.

In this period England was a land of unparalleled prosperity and the newly rich were keen to visit gardens at home and abroad. The Grand Tour became a required element in any young gentleman's education; new money could be clothed in the respectability of a collection of classical sculpture, and to house it perhaps a new wing could be added to your home, designed, of course, by the Adam brothers. Later in the eighteenth century owners of properties whose landscapes had been improved by the 'magician' Brown or by Humphry Repton were glad to let the public drive around their estates, and be impressed by the owner's wealth and good taste. At Stowe in Buckinghamshire so numerous were the visitors it was necessary to produce the first guidebook to a garden.

Jane Austen, with a characteristically sharp eye, saw what was happening and mocked the pursuit of fashionable landscaping in *Mansfield Park*. Mr Rushworth, wealthy, brainless victim of fashion, has been visiting a friend who has had 'his grounds laid out by an improver', a landscape artist such as Humphry Repton. (According to the historian J.H. Plumb 'improvement' was the most over-used word in eighteenth-century England; it was used with reference not only to parks and landscapes but to education, morals and agriculture.) Mr Rushworth is so excited by the idea of having his own estate 'improved' that 'though not saying much to the purpose, he could talk of nothing else'. During their visit to Rushworth's 'improved' estate the central characters of the novel emerge with particular clarity; Fanny is all stillness and acceptance, while Miss Bertram, when confronted with a locked gate, experiences 'a feeling of restraint and hardship. "I cannot get out"', she exclaims, and finds a way of squeezing past it. Here, as is by no means uncommon with works of art, the fictional visitors do not so much 'read' the landscape as they are 'read' by it. Contemporary visitors are also 'read' by the gardens they see; their reactions will tell us much about the kind of people they are.

In *Pride and Prejudice* several garden visits occur, and two are particularly significant. First, Elizabeth goes to stay with the insufferable Mr Collins and his patient wife, Charlotte, *neé* Lucas, who married only because being a bride was, in Austen's acid phrase, 'the pleasantest preservative from want'. When they enter the garden, Mr Collins leads the way 'through every walk and cross walk, and scarcely allowing them an interval to utter the praises he asked for, every view was pointed out with a minuteness that left beauty entirely behind'. Here we come to understand many of the problems attached to a guided garden visit, a point we will come back to. Later in the novel, with her aunt and uncle, who is 'in trade', Elizabeth goes to visit Darcy's country seat, Pemberley. First, they are shown the house by the housekeeper, who is full of praise for her employer. The park Elizabeth has already admired – 'She had never seen a place for which nature had done more, or where natural beauty had been so little counteracted by an awkward taste.' She is beginning to 'read' the man who owns these grounds and to see him differently, to realize there is little of artificial pretentiousness or hauteur about him, whatever the attractive Wickham might have said and she have previously thought. Garden design here is an important clue to character.

In the spring of 1786 Thomas Jefferson came to visit English gardens, notebook in hand. He was concerned with practical matters: 'my enquiries were directed chiefly to such practical things as might enable me to estimate the expense of making and maintaining a garden in that style', meaning the informal English style. At Chiswick he observed: 'the garden still shows too much of art. An obelisk of very ill effect; another in the middle of a pond – useless.' His 'romantic' nature objects to too much 'art', and his utilitarian American side finds fault with whatever is 'useless'. And Woburn in Surrey, the celebrated *ferme ornée* made by Philip Southcote in mid-century, he thought 'merely a highly-ornamented walk through and round divisions of the farm and kitchen garden'. Yet when Jefferson came to make his own garden on a hilltop at Monticello, he created a walk ornamented with flower beds, overlooking his vegetable garden, so perhaps he had learned something.

In the nineteenth century, garden visiting continued to grow, and owners of gardens made fashionable by the new horticultural magazines had even to provide waiting rooms for their visitors. At Biddulph Grange in Staffordshire entry was free on the first Monday of every month during the summer; at other times the charge was five shillings (25 new pence), a not inconsiderable sum, perhaps designed to keep out the riff-raff. The garden was closed on Sundays, naturally.

In the twentieth century the inter-war years gave many weekenders the opportunity to visit the gardens of virtual strangers, and to sneer at them. Nancy Mitford's semi-autobiographical *The Pursuit of Love* takes its narrator to the weekend retreat of the wealthy Kroesigs (their name says it all):

> The garden that lay about it [the house] would be a lady watercolourist's heaven, herbaceous borders, rockeries, and water gardens were carried to a perfection of vulgarity, and flaunted a riot of huge and hideous flowers, each individual bloom appearing twice as large, three times as brilliant as it ought to have been, and if possible of a different colour from that which nature intended. It would be hard to say whether it was more frightful, more like glorious Technicolor, in spring, in summer, or in autumn. Only in the depth of winter, covered by the kindly snow, did it melt into the landscape and become tolerable.

Like the house, which was furnished 'neither in good taste nor in bad taste, but simply with no attempt at taste at all', the garden is made to reveal the owners as 'outsiders'. A parallel example from life, not fiction, is provided by James Lees-Milne's diaries. On 6 August 1947, together with Harold Nicolson and Vita Sackville-West, he visited Littlecote in Wiltshire; this is his comment: 'The place was purring with gardeners, but very much a rich man's garden, tastelessly laid out.' Taste, whatever the word means (we will come back to it), has always been a marker of class to the English.

Serious twentieth-century gardeners went visiting not to sneer but to learn, as did Vita Sackville-West. After a visit to Nymans in the Sussex Weald in 1954 she writes: 'One can learn so much by visiting a garden such as this; it offers a short cut to hard-won experience. How bitterly I regret that thirty years ago I never had the sense or the nous to go and look at what other people had done and had planted, but just blundered on in ignorance, losing valuable years which could never be made up in terms of growth.' At Hidcote in Gloucestershire she saw a group of *Primula* 'Garryarde' 'as big as the largest lettuces. I blushed as I looked at them, remembering my own poor starved samples'; gardeners inevitably make comparisons between their own plot and that being visited, and envy is often the result. Her experiences of the great gardens of Cornwall were also learning experiences which 'may arouse envy, but they certainly destroy self-satisfaction'. This feeling of envy is common among garden visitors who are gardeners. Jamaica Kincaid in her stimulating *My Garden (Book)* finds herself constantly envious in the gardens she visits, but this envy stimulates her to further efforts in her own garden. She knows she will never achieve the garden she has in mind, but that again is good because 'a garden should never satisfy. The world as we know it, after all, began in a very good garden, a completely satisfying garden – Paradise – but after a while the owner and the occupants wanted more.' Perhaps as a result of original sin, gardeners always want more, particularly more of what they see in other people's gardens.

Margery Fish was another who wrote of the value of garden visiting: 'We all have a lot to learn and in every new garden there is a chance of finding inspiration – new flowers, different arrangement or fresh treatment of old subjects. Even if it is a garden you know by heart there are twelve months in the year and every month means a different garden, and the discovery of things unexpected all the rest of the year.' It should be added that to learn like this requires a mind open to new possibilities, with no rigid set of self-satisfying rules about what constitutes good taste or successful planting. Rosemary Verey was pleased with her borders at Barnsley House in Gloucestershire until she visited Great Dixter in Sussex in the company of its owner, Christopher Lloyd. 'As I walked round his borders with him, my pride-bubble burst', she candidly admits; 'Christo [Lloyd] had the edge on us with his clever use of unusual annuals and biennials.' The comparison of one's own garden with that being visited is not always comforting, if one visits with an open mind.

And in the early twenty-first century what is the picture of garden visiting in the United Kingdom? The National Gardens Scheme, which raises money for various charities, now has 3,700 gardens in its *Yellow Book*, and these are visited by about half a million people a year. Over the last ten years the NGS has raised more than £25 million, so clearly visiting gardens is a popular pastime. And having a *Yellow Book* garden may add not only to your prestige but to the value of your house, so that many garden makers are keen to join the scheme. The vague criterion for inclusion is that your garden should offer forty minutes' worth of interest to a visitor. Which, of course, begs many questions: 'Which visitor?',

'With what interests?' and 'At what time of year?' are just a few. Charles Elliott, like Henry James an American transplanted to England, thinks he knows what persuades so many people to visit gardens. 'Most garden visitors are gardeners,' he writes. 'There's no point in being too snooty about it – we traipse around in a haze of admiration and envy and (most likely) the conviction that there, but for the ungraciousness of God, go we.'

Too seldom garden visitors think about what they will wear during their visit. At the most they don comfortable shoes if there will be much walking, and put on a mackintosh if rain seems to threaten, but how often do they think of the colours in which they dress themselves? Some glaring colours can ruin the enjoyment of other garden visitors. And we might remember, too, the sensibilities of the garden owner. Beatrix Farrand, reporting to the board that ran her home at Reef Point in Maine, wrote: 'Those who see the garden's visitors from the windows wish that fashionable scarlet coats would not pause too long minutes in front of lavender and pale pink flowers – but mercifully fashions change.' She was thinking, surely, of the fashion in clothes rather than the fashion in plants.

Great Dixter, Northiam, England

Learning, comparing, admiring, envying, seeing (perhaps even noticing), smelling, listening, garden visitors – whether gardeners or not – clearly find something in gardens that other works of art do not provide. But how are gardens best visited? In guided groups (often the only way to see private gardens), alone or in the company of a friend? Guided visits are usually the worst; too often they suffer from the Mr Collins syndrome (see above), particularly if the guide is the garden's owner or maker. We are told what to look at, what to admire, how to react – which sometimes provokes in the recalcitrant visitor the opposite response from that the guide demands. And a guided visit in a group is often full of frustrations: the guide cannot be heard, or the space is too narrow so the audience spreads on to the flower beds, or one member of the party is continually asking plant names, so your tour is slowed to a snail's pace. Gardens are best explored, 'read', experienced alone. When faced with a choice of paths, you can then take the one that appeals more to you, the one down which the garden seems to be beckoning you. You can spend as long as you like in front of a particular border, and speed past a collection of plastic sculpture you find repellent. Above all, you can concentrate on the experience the garden is creating in you. But if you can find a friend to visit the same garden on the same day, someone who will take their own route, and then meet you afterwards, you will benefit from another eye appreciating things you may have missed, so your experience of the garden will be the richer.

3 THE GARDEN CRITIC

'There are two kinds of critic . . . there's the appreciator (who says, "You really must see this, it's terrific"), and there's the adjudicator (who says, "I really wonder if this is worth seeing at all"). They are both necessary.'

Seamus Heaney

Garden visiting, as we have just seen, has long been a popular pastime, and, like so much else, it has recently gone global; international garden crawlers now need guidance on where to find the best gardens. In the UK *The Yellow Book*, published by the National Gardens Scheme, and *The Good Gardens Guide* are essential tools for the garden visitor. But what about Europe and further afield? *The Good Gardens Guide* used to dip a cautious toe into what some English still call 'the Continent', but limited itself to gardens within easy driving distance of the Channel Tunnel; now it does not stray so far afield. Increasingly guides are available to gardens in European countries and in the parts of the Commonwealth where garden fever followed the flag, but they are harder to find in China, Brazil or India, although all these countries have notable gardens. Even when there are guidebooks, they usually contain information on where to find the garden, opening times (more often than not, out of date) and descriptions of some of the things we will find once we get there, but there is little in the way of judgment on the quality of the garden.

True, *The Good Gardens Guide* awards one or two stars to British gardens it considers of exceptional merit, although its criteria are never made very clear. And on the other side of the Channel the DRAC – the Direction Régional des Affaires Culturelles, a branch of the French intellectual bureaucracy – awards the classification '*Jardin remarquable*', according to precisely defined criteria: the composition of the garden, the way it integrates with its site, the presence of 'remarkable' elements, botanical interest, historical interest and quality of maintenance. The award of this accolade lasts only for five years; then the garden must be re-assessed. Here is a laudable attempt to take the art of gardens seriously, although pragmatic Anglo-Saxons will probably mock at the union of bureaucracy and aesthetics. But in most countries, other than the UK, there is no guide to the best gardens, which can be tucked into the glove compartment beside the Michelin restaurant guide.

In the United Kingdom there is, perhaps, a fear of the word 'critic' because the verb 'to criticize' carries implications of finding fault. Yet the fearless and forthright Gertrude Jekyll subtitled her book *Home and Garden* 'Notes and Thoughts, Practical and Critical, of a Worker in Both'. Writing of literary criticism, Dryden addressed the misunderstanding of the word 'critic' with exemplary clarity: 'They wholly mistake the nature of criticism who think its primary business is to find fault. Criticism as it was first instituted by Aristotle was meant as a standard for judging well, the chiefest part of which is to observe those excellencies which should delight a reasonable reader.' For 'reasonable reader' let us substitute 'reasonable garden visitor'.

For the contemporary writer Noël Carroll in his book *On Criticism*, the main role of the critic is also 'judging well', or as he puts it 'evaluation'. In order to reach a just estimate of the work in question (he is writing mostly about criticism of the fine arts), he argues that the critic must do four things before coming to a judgment of the work's value: describe, classify, contextualize and interpret. How might this work in garden criticism? Description is easy, and is what we find is most garden writing. Classify? We need to decide what kind of garden we are looking at, so as to be sure we are judging the work by appropriate standards; thus a Japanese dry garden should not raise the same expectations as an English flower garden, nor an Islamic garden be directly compared to a garden of the Italian High Renaissance. By 'contextualize' Carroll means placing a work in its historical setting, so that, again, we do not apply inappropriate standards – expecting, for example, a wide range of plants in the recreation of a sixteenth-century garden. Finally the critic will interpret the work, showing what seem to him or her the intentions that lie behind the design of the garden, and what it reveals of the character of its maker. Only then will it be possible to come to some kind of critical judgment of what the critic has been seeing. If we accept this definition of the critic's role, surely no rational garden owner could protest at, let alone fear, a critical appraisal of his or her creation.

In the UK the absence of criticism (not in the sense of carping fault-finding, but in the sense of intelligent evaluation and sensitive assessment) seems all too common in garden writing also. Articles in the garden press are often factual, listing plants, describing (sometimes gushingly) the look of the garden on the day the writer visited and reporting what the owner said. We have literary critics, drama critics, music critics, art critics, even restaurant critics; in these arts the critics provide a useful service, not only informing us about what is new and what is available but also offering some kind of judgment on the worth of what they have seen, heard or tasted. They begin the process of sorting the good from the excellent, the mediocre from the bad; they aim to detect the pretentious, the plagiaristic, the superficial. As readers of this criticism, we do not necessarily accept every judgment, but we will find ourselves stimulated into defining our views and judgments more exactly; we may also have our eyes opened to meanings and beauties we had not previously detected, and will thus value the experience of the artwork more highly. And if, as François Truffaut suggested, taste is the product of a thousand small distastes, then even from a disagreeable experience our ideas will emerge more defined, even, perhaps, more refined. As the great Humphry Repton wrote: 'The man of good taste endeavours to investigate the causes of the pleasure he receives, and to enquire whether others receive pleasure also.' Why, then, should we not ask what it is in a garden that gives us pleasure and what we dislike, thus taking a small step towards becoming garden critics?

One problem for the garden critic is the instability of the garden experience, though the same might be said of a single performance of, for example, an orchestral work. Among works of art, gardens are the most subject to time and to other forces outside the maker's control. We can put a mark on a canvas in exactly the place we want it to be, and the colour is also entirely in our control, though here, too, time may make changes; similarly, the composer can call for a particular chord at precisely the moment he or she requires it. The film maker and the editor control the precise angle of a shot and the length of time we are allowed to see it. But gardeners may find that the grey-leaved artemisia we planted to harmonize with the rest of the herbaceous border will not grow in our soil, or that moles have undermined it or bugs have blighted it – and then there is the problem of its yellow flowers. But in a great garden like Sissinghurst in Kent everything will have been taken into account – there will be spare plants to replace the blighted, and the yellow flowers will either take their place in a new composition or will be cut off. Though few private gardeners can aspire to these heights, we can enjoy the excellent – in composition and in maintenance – when we see it.

A second kind of instability is that gardens grow not just in a season but over the years; like their owners and creators, they are young and gangly, afflicted by middle-aged spread and then blowsily old. The crisp proportions of an *allée* will become blurred with the years unless there is a rigorous programme of pruning; shrubs will lose their shape, and planting schemes their proportions as the more thuggish plants assert themselves. But there is no reason for the garden critic to give up in the face of all this flux, any more than a theatre critic should give up because he has seen only *a* performance of *Hamlet*, not *the* performance that Shakespeare himself intended, or a music critic should give up because he has heard a performance of the Mozart Requiem that was far from perfect in all its parts.

Certain things can be relied on to give almost every garden visitor enormous pleasure at any time. For example, at Knightshayes in Devon the juxtaposition of the highly coloured, low-growing plants in the open garden beneath the walls of

Knightshayes, Tiverton, England

the house and the enclosed, green garden beside it, which contains only a circular pool with water lilies, a stone bench, a statue and a silver pear. The contrast is deliberately, even shockingly, dramatic, but (as with so many good works of art) after the shock of surprise comes the peace of understanding.

Garden photographs, which mouth-wateringly decorate so many articles about gardens, are always misleading in their stillness and permanence. They can take no account of the complex experience of being in a garden – the proportions of the spaces into which the garden is divided, the smells, the sounds, the relationship of one part of the composition to another, the sense of process and imminent change, the fragility of the whole experience. And another thing: often photographs in garden magazines and books are no more than beautiful photographs taken in a garden; they make no attempt to show the garden's design and its characteristic excellences and faults. Thus they reveal more of the skill of the photographer than of the garden maker. Misleadingly, photographs of gardens imply that gardens should be looked at like pictures, but most gardens (perhaps one should make an exception for some Japanese gardens) are more like sculpture because the point of view is not controlled by the artist; the viewer walks round exploring the work from different angles as he or she chooses. For sure, the designer of the garden will want to draw attention to some particular part of the whole, so a carefully sited bench will tempt the visitor to stop and admire a thoughtfully organized composition, or a hole in a hedge will invite the eye to see a part of the garden as a picture, framed for a moment, before the visitor passes on.

Another way in which photographs of gardens can mislead is by suggesting you can achieve the impossible – impossible in your climate, in your soil, or just impossible. The book about the Prince of Wales' house and garden at Highgrove contained a delicious photograph of some dark tulips (probably 'Queen of Night') growing in the meadow that Miriam Rothschild had helped the Prince create. How many people must have been encouraged to try growing tulips in their own areas of wild grass! But what the photograph did not tell, because a single photograph cannot show time and process, is that the next year almost none of the tulips came up; these pampered beauties were no fit competition for the true meadow plants and the grasses that swamped them.

And yes, of course, there are many kinds of good garden, but there are also many types of good building, and of good novel; the architectural critic and the literary critic do not throw in the towel as a result. Nor is this a reason to close

Above and below Renishaw Hall, Sheffield, England

down the critical faculty when we see an interesting garden and just fall into a swoon of admiration without any attempt to understand what the garden means, why it is designed as it is, what it tells us of the period or culture that created it, what it may reveal of its creator and what makes it so memorable, so 'remarquable'.

Like the critics of other arts, garden critics must know their subject; they will need to know something of the history of the country they are visiting, something of the social context in which the garden was created, something of the history of taste that guided the designer. In China, for instance, it is necessary to have some understanding of Chinese social history to appreciate the different qualities of a scholar garden in Suzhou and an imperial garden in Beijing. And, as with any criticism, wide experience of different kinds of garden in many different parts of the world will help to make the critic's judgments more substantial and persuasive. Like all works of art, gardens will often reveal something of the character of their creator, and the garden critic will be alert for signs of an idiosyncratic personality in a garden. For example, the garden critic visiting Renishaw, the family home of the Sitwells in Derbyshire, will appreciate exactly the challenge that Sir George Sitwell was stubbornly throwing down to designers of the very late nineteenth century. On a hillside looking out over the Derbyshire coalfields, Sir George built a carefully symmetrical garden in imitation (perhaps even pastiche) of the great Renaissance gardens of Italy, a taste that had dominated a previous generation but was by then becoming outmoded; with its terraces, statuary, pools and fountains it seems curiously anomalous not only in its period but in its setting. Gertrude Jekyll was invited to suggest some of the planting for the borders at Renishaw, but the symmetry and architectural formality here are strikingly out of step with the gardening she was doing at Munstead Wood, where drifts of plants were interfused and the blending of colours was of supreme importance. Unsurprisingly Sir George did not accept her suggestions. With an eye trained by experience and reading, at Renishaw the garden critic will not just see the garden, but will understand the challenge Sir George was throwing down to contemporary taste, and sense something of his intransigent character.

Any critic's judgments are, of course, relative, not absolute – relative because of his or her own background, education and character; relative also because any critic may have visited the garden only once, at a particular moment of the day, in a particular season of the year. But there will be some criteria, certainly personal and initially undefined, that will remain largely unaltered, and thus certain questions will be fundamental in reaching an informed judgment of any garden's merits. First, there will be the question of how (if at all) the garden relates to the house – concealing it, setting it off, distracting attention from it; and then of how the garden relates to the landscape that surrounds it – is it a stepping stone into the beauties of the natural landscape, or is there a hard frontier, such as a fence, wall or ha-ha, between garden and landscape? In Japanese houses, the walls made of paper screens can be pushed back so that the garden and the house are almost united. Other gardens – Stourhead in Wiltshire is a famous example – turn their backs on both house and landscape; they suggest a paradise that is not of this world. In a celebrated Californian garden, Filoli, the fine house is set at one end of the long, narrow garden, but not looking down its length, instead facing out into the wilderness across a meagre terrace; the garden climbs the hill in a long strip away to the left, so that from the windows of the house you see little of it, and the formal gardens do little to enhance the beauties of the building. What a wasted opportunity, the visitor may think, but perhaps this design decision tells us something about the close relationship between Americans and their wilderness.

Second, the critic will look at the layout of the whole garden and consider the proportions of the spaces into which it is divided, for gardens are, in part, architecture. If these spaces are all roughly the same size or shape, there may be a sense of monotony. The critic will then ask how are these divisions achieved – using, for example, trellis, walls, hedges (formal or informal), even roses growing along rope swags. Is this the best way to divide this particular garden? Rope swags allow the eye to stray beyond the enclosure they flimsily define; walls prevent the eye from straying but may be claustrophobic. Sometimes an opening in a hedge or wall allows the visitor a tempting glimpse of what is to come; in Chinese gardens windows often have delicately carved tracery in an elaborate pattern, so that they not only frame beautiful compositions but are beautiful in themselves. The garden critic will ask if this device of partial revelation is well used.

And there will be questions about the variety of the spaces: are they all the same shape , treated in the same way, using the same plants; do they all have the same atmosphere? Think of the dramatic effect achieved at Hidcote when you leave the claustrophobic 'heat' of the red borders and climb the steps between the two summer houses: to the left is the cool, wide, green walk leading to open fields, to the right a narrow opening in the hedge leads to the Theatre Lawn, ahead is the French-style Stilt Garden; all three choices of direction offer open, green spaces to contrast with the almost crammed intensity of the colour we have just left behind. The divisions of the garden can also provide the psychological security of a repeated theme, together with the interest of variation that any successful work of art requires. At Hidcote, again, the layout of garden rooms establishes a theme, and makes us aware of the controlling hand of a consummate designer (and perhaps something of his shy character), but the garden rooms are vastly different; think of the circular, raised swimming pool jammed into a space apparently much too small for it, and, for contrast, Mrs Winthrop's Garden with its low planting and restricted colour scheme. At Hidcote we can also escape from rigidly planned garden rooms into the Stream Garden with its winding path and lush, free planting. One of the most dramatic contrasts comes after the Stilt Garden and its tightly pruned, rectangular lime boxes on straight trunks; what could be more formal, more French? Then a fine pair of gates, leading to what? The answer is extraordinary – to nothing, just a sweeping view of the Cotswold escarpment. You have escaped the garden with its controlled delights, and are invited to take a deep, relaxed breath of Severn valley air.

Theme and variation can be expressed in many other ways – paving, planting, hedges, colour schemes. The famous Red Garden at Hidcote and the equally famous White Garden at Sissinghurst establish a colour theme that is very powerful. But each demonstrates that it is not enough merely to mass together plants of the same colour if one is to achieve a fine effect; repeating the same plant to establish a theme is also important, and paying attention to the shape of the planting. The white border at Brook Cottage, Alkerton, in Oxfordshire, is one that lingers in the memory; here the perfect combination of plantswoman and architect (remember the Sackville-West/Nicolson combination at Sissinghurst) created a white border that was supremely well designed, with the plants repeating each other (but not too often), and grouped in such a way that the visitor could appreciate the individual beauty of their form and, at the same time, their contribution to the composition as a whole.

If theme and variation are essential in any work of art – the stability of fulfilled anticipation working hand in hand with the drama of surprise – suspense is also something the garden critic will look for in a good garden. All will not be revealed at once, but there will be tempting hints of what is to come – through gateways, over hedges, round corners. And there will often be a choice of paths to follow, each suggesting a different kind of anticipated pleasure. The visitor will be lured into an exploration of the garden by the feeling that

The White Border, Brook Cottage, Alkerton, England

there is something more to see, until finally the whole composition is revealed
and a tranquil sense of completeness achieved. Exploring a good garden is like
reading a good novel; we need interest and tension to keep us turning the pages
and at the end a feeling of satisfaction that all the subplots have fallen into place
as necessary parts of the whole.

The movement from light to shade and vice versa provides one sort of drama.
In Mediterranean countries and the tropics this is particularly true, but even
in England (when the sun shines) it is sometimes possible to achieve this kind
of excitement. At Snowshill Manor in the Cotswolds, for example, there is a
marvellous sequence that starts on the lowest terrace of this wonderful garden.
The sun-filled space is surrounded by high walls, and the claustrophobic feeling
of enclosure is intensified because the beds on each side are raised and stuffed
with plants. On one side an ancient barn with a heavy, Cotswold-stone roof
sweeping low is mysteriously dark; just in front a small pool reflects the light
blindingly. Escaping the dazzling sunlight, you enter the cool darkness of the
barn and for a moment can see nothing; then it becomes possible to make out
a doorway in the opposite wall. From here a path leads through a tunnel of

Viburnum opulus, underplanted with ferns and hellebores; the sunlight filters through the branches, dappling the ground with a shifting pattern of leaves, and the smell of damp earth is richly refreshing. At the end of the path a flight of steps leads up and back into the sunlight of the garden. Here another surprise awaits; to the left the view opens, breathtakingly, on to a steep hillside which sweeps down and away to distant Cotswold pastures. We have for so long been enclosed by walls and woodland that these contrasts – of light and shade, of enclosure and openness – are dramatically striking.

If water is used in the garden, the critic will ask if it is used to its full advantage. Water is such a powerfully emotional element that it is rarely insignificant in a visitor's garden experience. To see water put through its paces most thoroughly it is necessary to visit the Villa d'Este in Tivoli, just east of Rome. Here water moves up, down, sideways; in sprays, in falls, in jets; it leaps down the banisters of stairs, curtains a shady grotto, even plays an organ (Montaigne found this organ irritating when he visited the Villa d'Este in the late sixteenth century because it played only one quavering note; now, however, it has been restored to its full glory). And at the bottom of the garden water lies still in rectangular pools, mirroring the sky, the organ fountain and the stately cypress trees. In Chinese scholar gardens irregularly shaped pools are often the central feature, the reflections in them creating a feeling of spaciousness, as well as an atmosphere of calm. Water can change the mood of any garden space; its sound can cool the air, hide unwanted noise, but also irritate and stimulate frequent visits to the lavatory. Water must be treated with respect; at its worst it sulks miserably at the bottom of a mean pool lined with black butyl, like a jewel lurking in a sack.

When Ippolito d'Este decided to use the water from the River Aniene for such frivolous delights as fountains and waterfalls, local farmers may have been outraged at the waste of this vital resource. In Islamic gardens also water is used with prodigal delight, to establish the fact that we are no longer in the desert but in a place that may give us a glimpse of paradise, since it contains all that the desert lacks – shade, fruit and pavilions for taking our leisure. The Acequia garden in the Generalife at Granada uses moving water with great delight, as it arches out of a procession of fountains along the length of the pool. In the great Moghul tomb gardens of India, fountains and reflecting pools cool the air and irrigate the fruit trees of the sacred precinct.

The critic will also want to consider the use of colour in the garden – is it

too strident, thus ruining the atmosphere of the place, are the combinations of colour harmonious, could there be more life, more imagination in the way colour is used, and so on? Kandinsky in his 1912 book *Concerning the Spiritual in Art* wrote, 'Colour directly influences the soul. Colour is the keyboard, the eyes are the hammers, the soul is the piano with many strings. The artist is the hand that plays, touching one key or another purposefully, to cause vibrations on the soul.' The critic will have to decide if a skilful artist has assembled the colours in the garden being visited, and what is the effect on the soul of the visitor. And if there are herbaceous or mixed borders, the critic will also want to consider the shape of the planting, something too often ignored.

Then the garden critic may consider the quality of what professional designers call the hard landscaping – the steps, the terraces, the paths, the walls. In the best gardens these are not only well proportioned but well made, and of an appropriate material – appropriate because they harmonize with the house or with the landscape; thus, in country gardens, local materials will usually be most successful. Where no stone is available, brick can be used to great effect. Not only do bricks come in an enormous range of colours but they can be laid in different patterns, each of which has a different psychological effect on the visitor. Bricks

Opposite and above Villa d'Este, Tivoli, Italy

laid end to end lengthwise point a direction imperiously, as at Tottenham Court Road underground station in London, where the frenetic commuter is hurried along the underground passages by this restless, relentless pattern. Fortunately he or she is saved on the platform, where the pattern changes. A basketweave layout, by contrast, suggests greater stability and is much more calm; bricks laid in a herringbone pattern suggest gentler, more dignified movement, like the wake of a boat passing through still water.

The critic should also be aware of the problems and advantages of the site – heavy clay soil that expands and contracts, sandy soil that retains no moisture, rocky terrain, steep slopes, strong winds (in seaside sites particularly) and so on. There may be views from the garden, but views often come with the penalty of exposure to high winds. And how is the view handled? Is it framed between trees or in an arch? Or is it left entirely open, in which case the panorama may be so immense and unfocused it loses any impact. Often a single tree planted near what seems to be the middle of a view is not an obstruction but serves to keep the view interesting to the householder; as you walk round the garden the view is seen in different ways, but always with one part obscured.

In the end the garden critic, having tried to understand the garden – its social context, its historical period, the character of its maker – will assess its quality overall but pay attention also to particular failures and successes. And to what end? First, as Dr Johnson said of the literary critic, 'to improve opinion into knowledge', and then to establish some personal standards by which gardens, including one's own, are to be judged. W.H. Auden in his inaugural lecture as Professor of Poetry at Oxford asked, 'What is the function of a critic?'; he was, of course, thinking of a literary critic. He then asked what the critic could do for him, and his answers seem to me to apply with equal force to what a garden critic can do for the garden visitor. The critic, Auden claimed,

> can do me one or more of the following services: 1. Introduce me to authors or works [we may substitute 'gardens'] of which I was hitherto unaware. 2. Convince me that I have undervalued an author or work [garden] because I had not read them carefully enough. 3. Show me relations between works [gardens] of different ages and cultures which I could never have seen for myself because I do not know enough and never shall. 4. Give a 'reading' of a work [garden] which increases my understanding of it. 5. Throw light upon the process of artistic 'making'. 6. Throw light upon the relation of art to life, to science, economics, ethics, religion, etc.

The capacious 'etc.' with which Auden ends is of particular importance if we want to see the garden as a work of art, not just a collection of plants. And if we do not look at a Chinese garden, for example, in the context of its culture, we shall never come close to understanding it.

ooooo

A critical eye will improve the pleasure of the garden visitor, and it will also be helpful to the garden maker, particularly when it comes to the assessment of his or her own garden. Most gardeners have an uneasy feeling about one or two areas of their home patch, a feeling perhaps that something is not quite right in the design of one part, or that another is dead for much of the year. But with practice in garden criticism it will be easier to pinpoint exactly what is wrong. It is not easy to see the defects in one's own work, but by training a critical eye on other people's gardens, where merits and faults are more easily identified, it will become possible to see where things have gone wrong and why. What is important is to understand the reasons why things please or displease; if we fail to grasp the causes of our satisfaction, the temptation will always be merely to copy planting details or to imitate furniture or buildings, which may look wonderful in someone else's garden but be grotesquely inappropriate in our own. To take an example from Sissinghurst: perhaps as visitors we have been impressed

Sissinghurst Castle, Cranbrook, England

by the classical simplicity of the narrow yew corridors, and as a result plant some at home; after years of patient waiting for the trees to grow, the effect is disappointing. And why? Because the function of the yew corridors has not been thought about. At Sissinghurst they constrict us and deprive us of any colour sensation, so that the next space that we enter seems more open and the colours more vibrant. If we want to achieve this effect at home, we will do better by not copying every detail of the Nicholsons' planting but by designing a different kind of cool, green space, which may suit our own garden much better.

Familiarity breeds content; so it is only with a critical eye that we can analyse what is wrong in our own creations. In England the traditional taste is that everything should be blurred, perhaps because of the muted, damp light of our island, although the word used by garden writers is not 'blur' but 'soften'. We read of hard edges being 'softened', of straight lines being 'softened', of brilliant colours being 'softened'. But is this really what we want? Certainly the great Christopher Lloyd did not want anything 'soft' when he shocked the gardening world by eliminating his venerable rose garden at Great Dixter, planting in its place astonishing combinations of bright colours and dramatic leaf forms. If 'softness' is really what we want, we are setting out on a difficult path, because what is 'soft' can quickly become sloppy; to keep the exact balance between informality and structure is no easy matter and requires constant vigilance. Most visitors will recall gardens that have grown blowsy, where informal 'softening' has swamped the structure, in the same way that middle-aged softening of the human belly conceals what is left of the muscle structure underneath. Gardens, too, fall into middle-aged spread and sometimes need to be toned up with crisp lines and severe pruning. The eye of the garden critic will quickly distinguish between where to be severe and where some gentle tidying up is all that is needed.

Then there may be parts of our garden composition that are weak – the entrance, for example. Like the first chapter of a good novel the entrance introduces us to a new world and whets our appetite to explore further; in Chinese gardens it often takes the form of an empty lobby between the urban world of stress and the peace of the garden. Another part of our composition may lack focus; perhaps it needs a bench or a statue or a pool. Or paths may dominate at the expense of the repose provided by open spaces. One famous private garden in the west of England feels like a maze, all hedges and paths; in the end the visitor wonders where the centre is, and what has been the point of following all these paths. Seats or benches can play an important part as focal points in a composition, and they can be beautiful in their own right; as well as things to look at, they are places to look from. Might they be better placed, or better made? In some gardens the borders are just that, mere fringes to the lawn or the paved area; they look mean and unhappy. But make them larger, with taller and bulkier plants, and they are no longer the sulky, shrinking apologies they at first seemed.

After looking at your own garden with the eye of a critic, you may decide that the whole space is just the wrong shape, too small or too flat. Don't despair. It is possible to play tricks with perspective so that a small garden can be made to look bigger; apparently parallel borders can gently and subtly converge, and the planting can be graded so that the biggest plants are closer, while similar but smaller plants are placed further away. Colours, or perhaps more accurately tones, can also be used to change the apparent shape of a space; brilliant tones seem to advance towards you, while muted tones recede. I remember a border in my own garden that troubled me; it was planted with wonderful white phlox, which loved the damp, heavy clay, but when they came into flower with their brilliant, pure white blooms, that part of the garden seemed to change shape, so strong was the advancing effect of the white against a dark, laurel background. If the site is flat, much can be achieved by subdividing it into garden rooms, and by varying the height of the plantings; even allowing grass to grow longer in places and then mowing paths through it will add to the interest.

A failing that the critic will often detect in the gardens of enthusiastic plant collectors is a restless lack of continuity; because the gardener cannot resist adding to his or her collection, many plants have been crammed in, and the border that results is spotty and speckled with specimens, like a museum showcase, not a work of art. Such a messy appearance can be corrected by repeating the plantings, or the colour patterns, and paying more attention to the shapes of the plants, thinking more like a sculptor and less like a curator. Again it is the artist's use of theme and variation that brings success.

To sum up, gardens can be 'read' like other works of art; they are the products of particular individuals living in a particular period of human history, and subject to the influences of a specific culture. To appreciate a garden it is important to know something of the cultural history that lies behind it – the aims that were common among garden makers in that culture, how they developed over time and so on. With this knowledge and a sharpened critical intelligence, the garden visitor will understand all gardens better, his or her own included, and thus gain more from the experience of visiting them.

4 THE GARDEN CRITIC IN ACTION

'The good critic is he who narrates his soul's adventures among masterpieces.'

Anatole France

So how might this garden criticism work in practice? How might it help us to get more from our garden experiences? Here are three reviews, which seek to understand the individual characters of three gardens, and then evaluate their particular virtues and weaknesses. The gardens discussed here have all been made in the last twenty-five years, and they are all open to the public on at least one occasion during the year. They were selected partly for their interest, but also because each has been celebrated by a certain measure of public acclaim. The northern garden, the Alnwick Garden, in Northumberland, was designed by an internationally celebrated team as a public garden; the eastern garden, the Old Vicarage, East Ruston, Norfolk, has been designed and created by the owners, as has the western garden, Veddw House Garden, Devauden, on the Welsh borders. *The Good Gardens Guide* rates the eastern garden at two stars (top rating), the northern and western gardens at one star. I visited each of these gardens, alone, in unexpectedly bright, sunny weather during June 2010.

The Old Vicarage, East Ruston, Norfolk
Alan Gray, one of the garden's creators, writes in the guide to this 32-acre/ 13-hectare garden: 'When we came here there was no garden at all, it was a blank canvas. This was no bad thing because it afforded us the opportunity to vent our creativity. Every part of the garden was designed entirely by ourselves as were all the various buildings. We have used no outside help, and our sole aim has been to try and enhance the setting of our home.' So they have pleased themselves and proudly take responsibility for all the design decisions. Laying out a garden in

The Old Vicarage, East Ruston, England

this part of England is not easy; there is a marked lack of natural features such as hills, woods and streams, which meant that the site made few demands around which the designers could organise their ideas; they had 'carte blanche' and such freedom is in itself a challenge.

The garden lies in the big-sky country of north-east Norfolk, only a mile and a half/2 kilometres from the North Sea. The surrounding land is intensively farmed, and as a result is there are few trees or hedges to break the power of the wind that whistles in from the north and the east. Thus the garden has to be protected by tree belts and high hedges (see photograph), which insulate it from the surrounding landscape, so that from the air it looks like an oasis in the flat, farmed landscape. The only features from outside the garden that play a part in its drama are the church towers and the lighthouse; following an oriental design tradition, these are 'borrowed' to be used as focal points for avenues and walks. All very traditional, and perhaps what one would expect in puritanical, conservative Norfolk. What you do not expect to find in a garden made by two local lads is a combination of outrageous glamour, dramatic theatrical coups and shocking colour contrasts. This is a garden that does not know the word 'moderation'.

THE GARDEN CRITIC IN ACTION

Left and right Two plant combinations at the Old Vicarage

Because the tree belts, acting as windbreaks, separate this garden from its surroundings, we might expect our entry into this magical world of artistic creation to take us by the throat; instead the entrance is rather drab and ordinary. We come first to a sales area where we get a preview of some of the rare plants to be found in the garden. It might be better if we left the garden through this area and entered it with more panache. But once inside there is no doubting that we have arrived in some special, exciting world. The gravelled courtyard in front of the house is filled with the rearing, contorted forms of black aeoniums, stately Melianthus major and huge phormiums – not what we expect to find in prosaic north-east Norfolk. Beyond this, we find the North Garden with shaded walks that curve; there are few curves in this ruthlessly rectilinear garden. Straight lines are emphasised by the parallel rows of trees in nearby Acacia Avenue. From here we escape into another set of parallel plantings in Holm Oak Walk; both avenue and walk end in roundels, so we are perhaps worried that there will be too much repetition in the shapes of this garden. Was this part of the garden laid out before more land was bought and the garden, or rather its designers, could stretch their wings in a more relaxed way?

Any fears of irksome repetition are soon quelled as we move into the Exotic and Sunken Gardens. The Exotic Garden sounds the keynote of the Old Vicarage – bold, even shocking, associations of colour and of leaf shape. The floppy leaves of banana and the giant leaves of stooled paulownia, scorching cannas and poisonous daturas make us feel we have reached a world far distant from the sugar-beet fields that lie outside the garden's boundary. Two raised pools cool the hectic colours and calm the bold, jungly effect of the leaf shapes, while their reflecting surfaces create a sense of space lest we feel claustrophobically overwhelmed. One of these pools contains a tall, vase-shaped fountain that shoots its water jets inward, to avoid splash when the winds blow. Such a dominant, man-made object is at variance with the mood created by the plants, and distracts attention from them. The Sunken Garden allows for a change of level rare in this garden. The guidebook tells us that this will be replaced by a rose garden, but not any old rose garden – 'It is our intention to make it quite spectacular, where roses will be combined with all manner of "different" plants, each complimenting [sic] the other in exciting new ways. It will be flirtatious, fun but above all else fabulous.' Here again we hear the authentic voice of the garden, although some visitors' epithets might be different - 'overstated', 'over the top', occasionally even 'overboard'.

What is wonderful about this garden, and also its gravest danger, is its lack of shyness, of restraint; it is 'in yer face' in a way that is very un-English. Most gardens in this country revel (if that is the right word) in muted tones and understated effects; harsh edges are 'softened' by planting, and colours are planned to blend gently into each other. At East Ruston, however, the colours often shout at each other; an example is the contest between a red heuchera and purple salvia seen in the illustration. Some will enjoy such effects; other will not. It is hard to remain indifferent to such daring planting. The designers are too subtle to allow such shock tactics to lose their effect by repetition, so, after the colour assault of the Exotic and Sunken Gardens, we are allowed a respite in the Green Court, which is planted only with monumentally still, fastigiate yews. A seat here allows time for us to draw breath before the next assault on our senses.

Not far away is another quiet area, the Tree Fern Garden. As in the Green Court, the sixteen dicksonias are planted in a formal pattern, and an underplanting of begonias, hellebores and aconites makes for interest in every season. The guidebook tells us that the tree ferns resemble 'the architecture of a medieval building'. They do not; they curve, bulge and cavort in a way that would make one fearful for one's safety if they were the columns supporting a roof. These monsters branch out at about the same height as the surrounding hedge, which rather blurs their effectiveness; were they either taller or shorter than the hedge they would make more impact. Indeed the hedges in the whole garden are uniformly tall, and this does make a visit sometimes feel a little like the exploration of a maze.

After these calm, largely green episodes, we are ready for another dose of heat. Not far away are the sweeping, parallel curves of the Mediterranean Garden, which gently descend in a series of fan-shaped, south-facing terraces to another green space. Here there are no hedges and no tall trees, but the same intense planting that we have come to expect – intense in its colours and in its density. Kniphofias we might expect and agapanthus, but the blue spires of *Echium pininana* and the arching, red necks of *Beschorneria yuccoides*, a Mexican native, may well take us by surprise. An oddity of the design here is that it is impossible to escape from the heat of the Mediterranean Garden into the green space of lawn beyond; we cannot move from one to the other, only look. At the end of this stretch of grass there is one of the few moments in this monastically enclosed garden when we are invited not only to look out from the garden but even to escape from it into the surrounding agricultural land – a footgate leads out into a sugar-beet field.

Another hot experience is offered by the Desert Wash, the most original and most successful part of the whole garden. Neither Graham Robeson nor Alan Gray, the garden's creators, has been to Arizona (they can have had little time for travelling since they began making this labour-intensive garden), but they claim that the landscape of the American south-west inspired them in making this garden. Here the rigidity of formal plantings and straight lines gives way to heaps of glaringly white, twisted, shiny flints. The odd, unpredictable angles of the stone both echo and contrast with the spiky planting of agaves, aloes and cacti, while startling colour is provided by drifts of the brilliant yellow eschscholzia. The contrast with the calm grass surroundings is dazzling and daring, as is so much in this shocking garden. There is also much relief in feeling that the garden has been allowed a bit of freedom after the imposed straight lines and formal plantings. But soon afterwards, the whip is cracked again and order restored with an avenue of not very happy *Trachycarpus fortunei* leading to a column that has been set up as an eye-catcher. There is sometimes too much of the ruler and the drawing board about this garden for all its opulent planting; perhaps this is a temptation when beginning from scratch on such a flat site.

In contrast to the bright jaggedness of the Desert Wash a woodland walk allows us some shade and the paths here wander informally through the undergrowth. A curiosity of this garden is that sinuous paths are found only in shade, here and in the equally shaded North Garden: is there something shameful about curves, so that they can be tolerated only when hidden modestly in shade? The Woodland Garden has some delightful foliage contrasts, and it provides a gentle relief after the dazzling, dramatic colours we find elsewhere. Sometimes this drama becomes a bit repetitive as we come across yet another eye-popping canna. Near the house the bright, hard yellow of *Cheiranthus cheiri* shouts for attention but draws the eye away from the other lovely plants. *Lobelia tupa* was about to bloom above this wallflower, and I wondered how its flowers of a restrained, dusky red would stand up to the competition. In this area we find again daturas, abutilons and acanthus. Will Alan and Graham one day use colour less shockingly, perhaps creating a garden with shades of the same colour? Probably not is the answer, since Alan tells me, 'The older I get the more

The Desert Wash, The Old Vicarage

outrageous I become.' His hope for the future is not to make the garden larger but to make it 'more intense, more interesting.'

This daring garden challenges the visitor to respond, careless of whether the response is favourable or not. If there is a flaw, it is the sense of repetition – the hedges all of the same height, the shock plants used too often, the straight lines.

The Alnwick Garden, Alnwick, Northumberland

This garden also turns its back on its surrounding landscape, neither the neighbouring castle nor the ancient town is glimpsed from any point in the garden. Only from the Woodland Walk and the entrance to the Treehouse can one get some glimpses of the park that 'Capability' Brown designed in the eighteenth century. From the enormous car park, for which, disgracefully, the visitor must pay, the garden is entered across a busy road. A sign telling coaches where they may allow their passengers to disembark prepares us for the fact that this is a public garden, a fact acknowledged by the guidebook which contains a foreword by the present Duchess of Northumberland, in which she writes, 'the Alnwick garden is a public garden for the twenty-first century, to be experienced and enjoyed by people'. She hopes the garden will be a 'fun' place, 'while also being a garden rooted in the local area and that Northumberland can be proud of.' When she uses the word 'experienced', I suspect she means 'used' rather than responded to with all the senses. This garden is public in another sense: though the Duke gave the site to the trust that runs the garden, much of the funding came from public sources, the Regional Development Agency and the Heritage Lottery Fund. It seems the former made a good investment since by 2008 it was calculated that the garden and its activities were contributing £6.9 million a year to the local economy.

The Alnwick Garden's website boasts that it is 'the most exciting contemporary garden on earth'. Yet it is a garden in only the broadest sense of the word, rather as zoological gardens are gardens. It would more accurately be described as a pleasure park, since at present there are only two areas where the interest is principally horticultural – the Rose Garden and the Ornamental Garden, though in spring the Cherry Orchard, planted with *Prunus* 'Tai Haku', the great white cherry, must be a delight. We have to say 'at present' because this garden is not yet finished; we are promised a spiral garden, a garden for the senses and a quiet garden. In the guide to the garden the Duchess comes close to admitting that this is not a garden in the usual sense of the word: 'To view

The Ornamental Garden, Alnwick, England

Alnwick garden as a showcase of design and planting is therefore a mistake. It's about people and was created to be experienced rather than looked at. I wanted it to be an inspiring resource for groups within our community and a garden that would appeal not just to the horticultural elite but also to both children and the elderly.' There are some strange assumptions and contrasts at work here: are the elderly never part of the horticultural elite, whatever that may be? Could not a beautiful garden, in the more usual sense of the word, also be 'an inspiring resource'? When we visit other gardens, do we not usually experience them rather than just look at them?

Numbers, particularly of pounds, figure large in the guidebook to this garden. The price of entry is high, at present £10.50, which includes a £1 donation to Gift Aid, and though the garden itself is a registered charity. Then there are said to be 16,500 species of plant in the Ornamental Garden – can this really be true? We are invited to sponsor a cherry tree – £250; a chair – £400; or a flower bed – £1,000. The Grand Cascade is built in 23 weirs; it carries 7,260 gallons of water a minute at peak flow, and 250,000 gallons are stored in the reservoir beneath. Last year the Alnwick Garden attracted 550,000 visitors.

It is no surprise then that we enter the garden through a visitor centre, a fine, airy structure by Michael Hopkins, which allows us plenty of shopping opportunities. Immediately we step out into the garden the Grand Cascade thumps us in the eye; it occupies the majority of the opposite hillside. For some reason it is constructed in a series of widening curves as it descends the hill. The arbitrariness of the design makes it seem clumsily inelegant. But perhaps it will seem less so when the area between the Cascade and the visitor centre is filled with a giant basin which will bring the waters of the Cascade right up to the steps we descend into the garden. In front of the Cascade was something that appealed much to the young: a collection of plastic dumper trucks, which they could ride around in, propelled by their own power. That these were bright yellow might offend some; it seemed to me quite in keeping with the jolly atmosphere of an entertainment park.

On either side of the Cascade curving, hornbeam tunnels lead up the hill to the gateway we have seen from the bottom. This is one of the few moments when we feel that one of the garden incidents is related to another, and that the design points the visitor the way to go. One blogger writes, 'The Alnwick Garden is just a bunch of unrelated stuff' – not very elegantly expressed, but he is right; it is a collection of poorly related incidents, with no narrative structure. Following these tunnels, we emerge at the top of the Cascade where a sturdy, Victorian triple stone arch welcomes us into the Ornamental Garden, which is of irregular shape and walled. Against the walls mixed borders are well planted with shrubs and ornamental plants, though the planting is too often in blocks of uniform size. Some thought has been given to colour in the planning, so pale yellow lupins show up well against the deep green leaves and blue flowers of a ceanothus. From a central raised pool water runs down the rills in which the young can (and do) play; all the streams are shallow enough for children to play in them safely. In the four corners well-made seats are embowered in pergolas, over one of which the rampant rose 'Paul's Himalayan Musk' clambers. The main part of the garden is divided into box-edged rectangular beds; the line of the box is echoed at a higher level by pleached crab apples, so that each bed is twice delineated, once at ground level and once by a mid-air cage. These stilted trees are an unusual and distinctly Continental touch, which is unsurprising given that the designers of the garden are the Belgians Jacques and Peter Wirtz – although the guide reminds us that 'The Duchess leads the design team.'

These central beds have an outer and an inner compartment. The outer,

View from inside a William Pye water sculpture, Alnwick

nearer the path, is usually planted with weed-suppressing geraniums and epimediums, together with euphorbias and alliums. Characteristically the plants in the inner compartments are of one type – here a bed of oriental poppies, there one filled with peonies. But what is to follow these displays? Cimicifuga in the poppy beds, asters and Japanese anemones in the peony beds – and it seems that that is all. There is a lot of immaculately clean earth, hoed, one guesses, by one of the ten gardeners, two apprentices and two students on placement. This is a high-maintenance garden with all the topiary, the box edging, the hornbeam tunnels and so on, but in a good garden how much time should be spent hoeing? The hoe is always the instrument of the gardener who prefers tidiness to serendipity; in its general massacre it leaves nothing to chance, because it spares nothing. In some of these carefully hoed beds standard roses are paired with currant bushes. Everywhere the labelling is very clear, although the labels that announce the availability of that plant in the sales area are not a happy touch.

Three other sections of the Alnwick Garden have achieved some kind of fame – the Serpent Garden, the Poison Garden and the Treehouse. The first of these has little to do with serpents, except that its paths wind sinuously; it is a garden

The Tree House, Alnwick

in which to display water sculptures by William Pye. These are beautifully made of stainless steel, and they are enjoyably interactive in the sense that you can get inside some of them (see photograph). The fun is mixed with education, almost inevitably these days; for example, the action of the meniscus is explained in a panel near the sculpture that displays the phenomenon. How many people read the panel?

The Poison Garden is also intended to combine fun and instruction: the garden is kept locked and visits can only be made with a guide. The most dangerous plants are grown in cages, and, wittily, visitors are counted in and counted out. Ghoulish descriptions of the workings of different poisons derived from plants appeal to some youngsters, and may warn them of the negative effects of drugs. The Treehouse is an enormous construction held up in the branches of fifteen mature limes. It comes equipped with a fully functioning restaurant, rope walkways and, astonishingly, wheelchair access. Another witty touch here: in the lavatory some plastic ivy twines around the downpipe before climbing up to the cistern.

The Alnwick Garden is what in America they call 'an attraction'; no wonder it gets enthusiastic praise from the web site called DAYoutWITHthe KIDS. It is completely child-friendly and there are no 'keep off the grass' signs. The elderly also seem to enjoy it. But there is one category who have been left out in this garden's planning, or left out so far – lovers. There is little romance about the place, and few private corners except the bowers in the Ornamental Garden, which are too huge to be intimate. The website gardenvisit.com is right in its review: 'The scale is not well-judged – it is too small to be awe-inspiring and too large to be charming.' But perhaps it is too soon to judge; the garden is due to be finished by 2015 and that will be the moment to come to some critical conclusions.

Veddw House Garden, Devauden, Monmouthshire

The contrast between the Alnwick Garden and the Veddw House Garden could hardly be greater. Veddw is a private garden made and designed by its owners, Anne Wareham and Charles Hawes, who have limited time for gardening and limited resources, with no support from public funds. It lies down a narrow lane, too narrow for coaches, outside the village of Devauden on the Welsh borders; there are no signs to help you find it. Another significant difference is in the attitude to weeds in the two gardens; if the hoe rules the Ornamental Garden at Alnwick, Veddw has a bold sign in the car park reading: 'WEEDS. If weeds really upset you, perhaps you'd best go home and save your hard earned cash. We garden to enhance the natural rather than to conquer it.' This garden challenges the visitor in many ways, and seeks to educate but in much subtler ways than Alnwick.

Whereas Alnwick Garden turned its back on castle and town, identifying itself as a twenty-first-century world-beater, the Veddw tells us something of the history of the locality, and the garden is only part of that story. Unlike gardens 1 and 2, this garden embraces its locality, both the geography and the history of the area; so the garden doesn't turn its back on its surroundings. Rather we are encouraged, often by intelligently sited benches, to look out at the landscape. People worked the land that is now a garden; they cultivated it to survive, and this is remembered in the 'That Population' Gate. There are several references to this agricultural past in the Veddw garden: one garden is called the Cornfield Garden, though it is now planted with grasses; another reproduces, in miniature, the 1848 layout of fields in the area. Then a bench records the different ways in which Veddw has been spelled at different periods of its history – the word means 'birch'. If Alnwick makes constant reference to the Duchess and to her generosity in giving her time free to the trust that runs the garden, Veddw might be described as an anti-aristocratic garden; its roots lie in the squatter populations who first worked the site. This thoughtful emphasis on place and history is unusual in a modern garden.

For all its humble origins the present garden at Veddw has been acclaimed as 'a garden of national status' and as one of the 'most influential and important gardens of the last ten years'. The Veddw House Garden is cradled in a fold of the well-wooded hills, with the modest house approximately halfway down the north-facing slope; just to the east lies the famous valley of the Wye, whose star attraction is Tintern Abbey. From the back of the house we look up the slope, along a central walk between tall yew hedges, which seem to enclose symmetrical compartments, and, above them again, to the beech woods that encircle this upper half of the garden.

The flat lawn immediately outside the back of the house is enclosed by the curves of symmetrical crescent beds. These beds are made hugely imposing because they are planted with tall things, including rosebay willow herb. This has the effect of shutting us in, but the enclosure is achieved by plants of the same

Veddw House, Devauden, Wales

height, and their small leaves, too, are all a similar size, which creates a sense of claustrophobic repetition. Such strong verticals can too easily suggest the bars of a prison. Moving up the slope between the yew hedges we are confident that we can 'read' the garden in terms of its formal symmetry, the paired crescent beds, the yew walk, and so on. Not at all! This is one of the delights of Veddw House Garden: you cannot 'read' it from a distance, and, if you try to, you will be mistaken. The yew hedges enclose spaces of different shapes and sizes, and each is differently filled. One of the most startling is almost filled by a shallow pool of water, dyed black (with an organic dye) so that it reflects perfectly the swelling curves of the hedges behind it - a design idea that is at the same time grand and very simple. A seat allows one time to sit and enjoy the reflections. Another enclosed space, named the Cornfield Garden, is elegantly paved in brick between beds filled with grasses, edged by rails carefully inscribed; the neat, four-square seats (from IKEA) are absolutely right here. But something has also gone wrong: this was the Cornfield Garden, planted with barley, but the barley failed. Yet the inscriptions still refer to farming and the growing of crops. This is a garden that does not mind admitting its failures. Perhaps we are reminded of Samuel

The Reflecting Pool, Veddw House

Beckett's immortal words: 'No matter, try again; fail again; fail better.'

Up the slope to the right of the yew walk lies an intricate pattern of box-edged beds filled with grasses. In an interview Anne Wareham says, 'I am not attracted to informal gardens with wiggly borders,' and certainly at the Veddw the structure is very strong. The grasses, untidily floppy by nature, are penned in by the box hedges, although some are so tall they threaten to overwhelm their confines. But this pattern of low hedges has another function than being beautiful: it reproduces the 1848 (the Year of Revolutions) Tithe Map of the area. 'Oh, yes, and so what?' might be the reaction. From the solid seat above, inscribed with the different spellings of Veddw, we look out at the surrounding landscape, but do not find the pattern of the beds echoed there. Nor is it easy to appreciate the pattern of the box-edged compartments. The writer Noël Kingsbury thinks the idea doesn't work: 'Nowhere is high up enough to read it [the pattern of beds] as a map, and many of the grasses are too large to be read as crops.' He is right; this part of the garden is controlled by an idea, not made to be beautiful, and the idea is not clearly communicated. Much of the garden at Veddw is acutely cerebral, perhaps too much so. But this pattern of beds is part of the garden's and the owners' history. Anne recalls that when she and Charles moved from London they found the landscape hard to understand, and to help her Anne began reading local history; 'At the same time I began to make a garden on the two fields which flanked the house.' The making of the garden and the understanding of local history occurred simultaneously for the garden makers, for this reason they used this pattern in their work of art.

Walking along the boundary with the woodland at the top of the garden, we notice the strange shapes made by the hedges, where they had once been cut-and-laid, but now the trees have been allowed to grow up again; the contrast between the horizontal of the laid hedge and the vertical of the re-grown trees is very striking. We pass the Addison Garden, and wonder why this area has been given a name that is so resonant in the history of English gardening. The answer is that he was one of Anne's ancestors. But that explanation leaves us feeling there is something uncharacteristically arbitrary in giving such a significant name to a small garden space. The woodland is very beautiful, in an almost oriental way, with its huge, noble beech trees underplanted (by nature or has there been a helping human hand?) with ferns among mossed boulders. Some periwinkle has escaped from the garden of the cottage that used to stand on the site, the ruins of which Charles and Anne have cleared, collecting shards of broken china, bottoms of bottles and rusted knives as they went. These clues to the garden's long history will, of course, be treasured and used in some way that has yet to be determined. Beyond the 'That Population' gate, with its long nineteenth-century quotation describing the legal status and living conditions of the squatters on the site, lies Charles' Wood. Here we find a single chair facing, but distant from, a television. Provocative. Witty. But what does it mean? Should visitors reflect on their viewing habits? Should we look at the wood in the same way we look at the TV? What are eyes for? Stop, enough! You begin to see how this garden works to challenge and disturb the visitor!

Below the house there is a formally-ordered piece of front garden to the left of the drive as you enter; box balls and a tall, rectangular beech arch give formal notice of entry into another part of the garden. And to the right a bed planted with the invasive, grey lyme grass, opposite a border of grey-leaved plants and then behind that a collection of grey and purple shrubs. There is, perhaps, too much purple, and too often it is used, banally, to contrast with grey. In Charles' Garden the gravel paths and the hard, bright light give an almost Italian feel to this colour-coordinated mixture of vegetables and ornamentals – more purple and grey here – and this brightness makes a dramatic contrast with the soft green of the meadow and the shady boundary walk under arching cotoneasters. The meadow where wild flowers flourish, orchids in particular, may be rather too unordered for the owners' taste, perhaps this is why they added a formal avenue of top-worked *Corylus avellana*, but, disappointingly, this avenue leads nowhere. In the beds of the Front Garden there is more purple, this time purple cotinus contrasting with the yellow hop, and in front of that the yellow loosestrife is set off by a purple-leaved lysimachia. Colour is not, perhaps, of the first importance in this garden, any more than flowers are; shape, space, dramatic layout and history are the things that really matter.

Anne has written: 'For the past fifteen years I have been making what I hope is a serious garden – in the sense that I hope it is worth taking seriously, even when it may entertain, amuse, or fail.' There is no fear of the critical eye in this fiercely cerebral garden; the criticism by Noël Kingsbury quoted above appears on the Veddw House website. And Anne is in the habit of asking visitors what suggestions they have for improvements. The present writer had three suggestions: 1. The crescent beds need more variety of height, shape and leaf size, so that the verticals are less oppressive. 2. A short flight of steps between two holly hedges are too wide for the space they occupy, an unusual error of judgment in a garden where proportions have generally been carefully considered. It turns out that these steps are the remnants of a much longer flight, which has now been abbreviated – showing how this garden (like most gardens) is still in the process of development. 3. The avenue in the Meadow should lead somewhere, perhaps through a gate or an arch into the shade of the Cotoneaster Walk.

This is a garden full of drama; there is almost always a choice of paths to take, each enticing us on with hints of interest just around the corner. It constantly take us by surprise – who could have expected a reflecting pool of such size in such a small yew enclosure? The plantings are bold – bands of hosta under a hedge, or foaming masses of *Alchemila mollis* twinned with blue campanula. As Anne writes in her notes on the garden, 'we are passionate about gardens, not about gardening', so the detailed maintenance is not of the highest order. But the important, structural things like the shape of the hedges are maintained to the highest standard. In Renaissance Italy gardens had meanings, told stories; Veddw House Garden, in its different way, invites a dialogue with the visitor, and this is a rarity in a twenty-first-century English garden.

ooooo

What have I been trying to do in looking at these three gardens in a creatively critical way? In general terms taking the gardens seriously; trying to respond to the particular character of each one, and then assessing what the makers were attempting to do, and where they have been successful and where they have failed. I have tried to respond to the special atmosphere of each of the three gardens, and to judge them without too much of the prejudice of individual taste. And taste is the subject of the next chapter.

5 TASTE

'A man of great common sense and good taste – meaning thereby a man without originality, or moral courage.'

George Bernard Shaw

Originally the word 'taste' referred only to sensations felt by the tongue; then, more generally, it began to refer to food or drink for which one had a liking, as in 'she has a taste for claret'. Only in the late seventeenth century did it come to mean 'mental perception of quality' or 'the power of discrimination'. In particular it came to refer to judgment when faced with questions of beauty in art or nature. In eighteenth-century Britain a person of taste became the model to which all educated people aspired. And what was taste? James Barry in his lectures on painting, delivered between 1784 and 1798, supplied a definition: taste is 'that quick discerning faculty or power of the mind by which we accurately distinguish the good, bad, and indifferent'. And who established what was 'good, bad and indifferent'? That was decided by those who dictated the fashion of the age. So the person of taste, then as now, was he or she who displayed obsequious obedience to the prevailing canons of beauty. We might wonder if there is no room for independence of thought and opinion where taste is concerned.

At the end of the eighteenth century the great garden and park maker Humphry Repton inveighed against what he called false taste:

> False taste is propagated by the sanction given to mediocrity . . . Its dangerous tendency, added to its frequency, must plead my excuse for taking notice of the following vulgar expression, "I do not profess to understand these matters, but I know what pleases me." This may be the standard of perfection with those who are

content to gratify their own taste without enquiring how it may affect others; but the man of good taste endeavours to investigate the causes of the pleasure he receives and to enquire whether others receive pleasure also.

We hear an echo of the false taste he castigates in the phrase still often heard, 'I don't know much about these things, but I know what I like.' It is, surely, to take the subjectivity of taste beyond rational limits to suggest that we can in no way account for what we like or why we like it, even when we have made no deep study of the subject. If we were never able to analyse the sources of our pleasure and displeasure, we could never imitate in our own gardens the beauties we admire in those we visit; we would only be able to reproduce them.

To see how taste changed in the eighteenth century and how it has constantly been changing since, here is Daniel Defoe in the 1720s describing what he considered the finest garden in the world:

> You descend from the Salon into the parterre, which hath a canal in the middle; on the right a wilderness, and on the left a fine green walk, which ends in a banqueting house. On one side of this green walk stands the greenhouse, finely adorned with statues, and uncommonly furnished with greens [meaning, at this period, not 'vegetables' but 'evergreen plants']; while behind this greenhouse are a variety of high-edged walks, affording delicious vistas. At the bottom of the canal is a bowling-green encircled with grottoes and seats, with antique statues between each seat; this bowling green is separated by a balustrade of iron from another green walk, which leads you to another long canal.

No mention of any colour except green, nor of flowers in harmoniously blended combinations, here at Wanstead, home of Sir Richard Child; no mention either of the ground rising and falling in picturesque undulations, nor of paths following sinuous curves; no Brownian clumps or tree belts; just canals, statues and greenery everywhere. Few English gardeners have this taste today, though the garden Defoe describes might delight a contemporary Italian. It might even be called tasteless to create such a garden in twenty-first century England.

ooooo

'There's no accounting for tastes' is a familiar saying, given more dignity when expressed in Latin – *De gustibus non est disputandum* (you can't argue about tastes). But there is only a grain of truth in these well-worn maxims. About some tastes there is, in truth, nothing to be said. Honey and a piquant cheese is a combination of flavours that appeals to some and not to others, and no amount of argument or explanation will alter the mind of the person whose palate is disgusted. No amount of argument, either, will persuade you that a 'New Dawn' rose of palest pink makes a fine combination with the jaundiced yellow of *Rosa* 'Whisky Mac' if you do not enjoy that particular combination of colours. However, it is sometimes possible to explain a preference, and to account for an aesthetic judgment in such a way as, perhaps, to persuade another person to share one's view, or, at least, to understand it better. If this were not so, literary criticism and other kinds of critical writing would be of little value.

Let us take an example. There are two famous gardens on the outskirts of Florence, one of which seems to me a failure as a work of art, while the other is a triumph. Both gardens feature in all the best guidebooks to Italian gardens – those of Helena Attlee and Penelope Hobhouse, for example. The guidebooks offer, rightly, almost no judgment of the merits of the gardens they include; rather they tell us what we shall find, and a little of the gardens' stories. The early history of the Villa Gamberaia is not entirely certain; the garden seems to have taken much of its present form in the eighteenth century, when the place was bought by the Capponi family. We know it was altered by the addition of pools of water, which replaced the flower or vegetable beds in the late nineteenth century; equally certainly both villa and garden were wrecked in the Second World War and restored by Marcello Marchi thereafter. The garden at La Pietra has a shorter history; the guidebooks tell us it was laid out in the early decades of the twentieth century by the Englishman Arthur Acton, very largely as a place to display his collection of sculpture. Helena Attlee does allow herself to hint at an opinion in the conclusion of her entry for La Pietra: having admitted it is a garden difficult to classify, and reflected on Acton's eclectic taste, she writes, 'The result is the kind of Italian garden one might see in a dream.' I wonder if she meant 'in a nightmare'.

Most writers on the subject of Tuscan gardens agree that both La Pietra and Gamberaia are of major importance. Ethne Clarke's *The Gardens of Tuscan Villas* boasts a foreword by Sir Harold Acton, son of Arthur and owner of La Pietra, who styled himself 'the last aesthete'. This is a book of photographs to which

Clarke has added a paragraph or two of the worst kind of gushing prose that sometimes disgraces garden writing, so vapid that its meaning is often impossible to elucidate. Here is part of what she has to say about La Pietra: 'Box and cypress perfume the air, convent bells, birdsong and the croak of frogs in the lily pond fill the garden rooms with quiet music; soft turf and hard gravel, warm stone and cool moss, shade and sun mark the progression from one heart-rending vista to another. This is a thoroughly sensual garden, paced to the contemplation of beauty.' On Gamberaia she is little better: 'Today,' she writes, with exasperatingly little detail, 'the gardens of Gamberaia provide the garden visitor with the most sublime pleasure and a profound insight into the history of Tuscan landscape design.' How much more sharply intelligent the brisk comments of Edith Wharton, written eighty-five years earlier: 'The plan of Gamberaia . . . combines in an astonishingly small space, yet without the least sense of overcrowding, almost every typical excellence of the old Italian garden: free circulation of sunlight and air about the house; abundance of water; easy access to dense shade; sheltered walks with different points of view; variety of effect produced by the

Villa La Pietra, Firenze, Italy

skilful use of different levels; and, finally, breadth and simplicity of composition' (*Italian Villas and Their Gardens*, 1904).

The gardens at La Pietra are currently the subject of a painstaking restoration to their 1930s condition and style. They are almost entirely green and white – the green (as if there were in truth only one kind of green) the colour of the cypresses, the box hedges and the sumptuous ivy; the white is provided by the balustrades, steps and statues that are everywhere in this peculiarly heartless garden. As Harold Acton writes in his foreword to the Ethne Clarke volume, Italian gardens 'depend mainly on their architectural design'. And it is precisely in this area that the gardens at La Pietra fail; the problem is that each of the spaces into which the garden is divided is so similar in proportions and style that the visitor never feels the pleasure of variety, nor the satisfaction of having reached the garden's heart. Not only that: each space is treated theatrically, with the same kind of cold, formal symmetry. But neither individual space nor the garden as a whole ever achieves grandeur, while at the same time failing to achieve a satisfying intimacy. This formality and lack of colour, you may say, is typical of the Italian garden style that Arthur Acton and his design advisers were attempting to imitate, or even recreate. True, but the great Italian gardens of the high Renaissance vary the dimensions of the spaces and their treatment. For example, the nearby sixteenth-century Medici garden at Castello has its great, sun-filled parterre laid out in patterns of straight lines, all to be appreciated from the *piano nobile* of the palace. But higher up the hill there is the *bosco* with its winding paths and shadows, and to one side the *giardino segreto*, walled and much more intimate in scale. At La Pietra we always feel we should move on – down some steps, along a path, through an arch – without ever feeling we have arrived.

And then the great Italian garden makers of the High Renaissance paid close attention to the proportions and details of their stonework – the rhythm of the balustrades, the proportions of steps, pools and so on. At La Pietra the steps are very sloppily handled, particularly those to the right of the terraces on which the garden is laid out. These ill-proportioned steps are not marked with a raised beginning and conclusion, so that they seem to slither out of the grass apologetically, like an indoor stairway leaving a landing. And instead of being contained within the bank they descend, they sprawl inelegantly out on to the terrace below. This handling of the hard landscaping is particularly difficult to ignore because elsewhere the topiary, typical of the classic Italian garden, creates sharp, elegant lines. This topiary and the hedges create contrasts of light and shade, as do the shadows thrown by the balustrading, but in all the spaces (or garden rooms, if you prefer) the proportions of light and shade are much the same. A visitor to Arthur Acton's La Pietra in the 1930s, Mabel Luhan, observed sourly, 'They say, my dear, you can buy anything in his villa if you want it.' The sculpture in the garden was also on sale; so perhaps La Pietra is an example of a garden as shop window, rather than a garden as work of art.

The garden at the Villa Gamberaia, by contrast, is a delight. The entrance drive, as at La Pietra, is lined with cypresses in the Tuscan style, but here the avenue is much narrower and strikingly tall, creating a sense of mystery and anticipation. Where it ends, in front of the house, visitors can turn left or right; there is only a lawn, no path to guide them. But most will turn right, and cross the grass to the balustrade that encloses the garden on that side, in order to admire the views of Florence, lying in the Arno valley below. From here the part of the garden we can see protrudes into the valley, completely flat, away to an apse of tall yew which marks the garden's limit; a window in the yew wall invites us to look out at a different view of the landscape below. As we are drawn towards the apse, we find, under the house, a completely symmetrical parterre of box and stately yews, with four water basins. Some rather feeble fountains make a weak, tinkling sound; pink roses and grey santolina set off the darker shades of yew and box. This parterre can best be enjoyed from the loggia in the corner of the house at first-floor level.

Rounding the end of the parterre, we see on the other side of the house an uninterrupted, flat lawn stretching an impossible distance into the hillside – impossible because this is the direction from which we entered the garden and there was never space for such a length of lawn. This is one of the great surprises of the garden, and is brilliantly achieved by extending the garden on a bridge above and beyond the road from which we entered. This lawn is called the Bowling Green, and at its end a grotto in the hillside bids us explore further. But as we set off down the long grass walk towards the grotto, an entrance on the right tempts us, unexpectedly, into a narrow garden confined by high walls of twisted volcanic rock, swagged with roses; here water once spouted out of a decayed statue at the back. Steep steps lead up into the dark wood of *Quercus ilex* that hangs over the garden on the right-hand side; on the left an identical set of steps leads up to a sunny space where lemon trees in huge terracotta vases are displayed outside the barn that houses them during the winter. And here a border of peonies luxuriates under the sunny wall. The

Villa Gamberaia, Settignano, Italy

visitor chooses to ascend into sun and colour or into shade under the drab green of evergreen oaks.

What makes the garden of Gamberaia such a delight? First, we feel we can take possession of it and explore it on our own terms; there are no paths to direct our feet, no arches framing views of the next garden room; rather we are left to wander over the grass as we wish. Then there are the contrasts – the openness of the long views and the enclosure of the yew apse; the sun of the parterre and the lemon garden set against the dark background of the *bosco*; the intricate patterning of the parterre with its pools contrasting with the simple unbroken stretch of grass that leads down to the nymphaeum, where the god Pan lords it over his kingdom. And the drama of the place, which at first seems so easily read and so predictable; the way we are tempted on to new delights we never suspected. Yet the whole garden seems to have happened, not been planned, and its small scale makes it particularly appealing; here is no swagger, no pretention, just domestic-scale delights.

Is this preference of Gamberaia over La Pietra solely a matter of taste? I would say rather it is a matter of rational judgment, the evidence adduced above proving the case. Gamberaia seems to me a better garden because it is a better work of art;

TASTE

like a good novel it is full of surprises but in the end utterly satisfying. Not that it has no faults; the box in the water parterre has perhaps been allowed to become too bulky and tall, but that is easily remedied. It is possible that La Pietra might seem delightful when the garden is full of people, but that will be because its defects are hidden. Certainly it will be improved by the current development of growing wild flowers in longer grass in some of the spaces; this will add variety of texture to the grass, and permit a few touches of colour.

○○○○○

Nothing divides one person's taste from another's more than the appreciation of a particular colour or combination of colours. Think of an alpine meadow in spring, full of the brightest, most various colours, but with nothing garish or discordant about them. These flowers are all the product of the same soil and the same growing conditions; maybe that is why (it seems to me) they harmonize so effortlessly. Perhaps William Robinson was thinking of an alpine meadow when he wrote sniffily of colour schemes: 'There is some talk of these nowadays. They need never be thought of, if we take good care to have good plants that grow in natural forms . . . in the garden the most beautiful colour can be got by natural ways.' Problems with colour began with the introduction of exotics and with the efforts of the hybridizers. John Parkinson, writing in 1629 with advice on how to plant a flower garden in England, makes no mention of colour combinations. However, as the garden historian Margaret Willes points out, Sir Henry Wotton praises the early seventeenth-century garden at Ware Park in Hertfordshire because its creator, Sir Henry Fanshawe, 'did so precisely examine the tinctures and seasons of his floweres that in their setting, the inwardest of those which were to come up at the same time, should be always a little darker than the outmost, and to serve them for a kinde of shadow, like a piece not of Nature, but of Arte'. It was the 'florists' of the later seventeenth century who were the first avid collectors of exotics, and as the British Empire spread so the British appetite for novelties increased. With the invention of the 'stove' or hothouse that appetite could be fed with even more rare specimens, sometimes of startling colour and form.

In the late sixteenth century enthusiastic gardeners began to experiment with hybridization, though their work was at first the subject of intense debate: was it right to interfere with God's handiwork, to make flowers larger and more colourful when nature had intended them to be demure and petite? These moral inhibitions soon gave way to human ambition. However, if one stands in front of a tree of that all too common cherry *Prunus* 'Kanzan' (also known as *P.* 'Kwanzan', *P.* 'Sekiyama' and *P.* 'Purpurascens'), it is possible to regret the hybridizers' ambition. This tree has the worst possible combination of colours in its bud, leaf and flower; the bud is maroon but the flower opens cyclamen pink, and, as if this vile combination were not enough, the leaf, too, is touched with red. Just a matter of taste? Perhaps, but it is hard to be persuaded of the beauty of this tree, at least as far as its colours are concerned. Is it beautiful in shape? Often no; its branches stand stiffly up and out from a trunk which is often ill proportioned when compared to the superstructure. Yet this tree is widely planted, and sometimes, to add to the horror, it is surrounded by daffodils of the most brazen yellow. William Morris had firm views on flowers produced by human will: 'There are some flowers (inventions of men, i.e. florists) which are bad colour altogether, and not to be used at all. Scarlet geraniums, for instance, or yellow calceolaria, which are not uncommonly grown together, in order, I suppose, to show that even flowers can be thoroughly ugly.'

If we agree that not all plants are beautiful in colour or in shape, then we will want to exclude some flowers and some shrubs from our gardens – and this is where taste begins. But even the plants we select for inclusion can be better or worse arranged, as the garden critic will be quick to notice. Graham Stuart Thomas, a gardener of genius, particularly in the creation of borders, writes: 'There is a difference of opinion about whether the colours of flowers clash in gardens. Here again it is a personal matter, but in my opinion it is a case of defeatism to claim that colours do not clash. It is an example of being careless and leaving to chance that which should concern us deeply.' 'Clash' here presumably means that the colours seem ugly in combination; they seem to fight with each other rather than harmonize. But might we perhaps want a little strife in our garden composition, a little of the energy that oriental garden makers achieve when they deliberately avoid a symmetrical arrangement of rocks, because it seems to them dead?

In a letter to Beth Chatto the late Christopher Lloyd, a man who loved lively colour combinations, takes up this point:

> Caryopteris, *Verbena bonariensis* and *Calamintha nepetoides* beneath them – all blue and purple. All very soft and harmonious, but devoid of bite, for my taste! It reminds me of Stephen Lacey's suggestion,

in my Exotic Garden, of partnering the *Verbena bonariensis* with *Thalictrum delavayi* and *Origanum laevigatum* 'Hopleys' – again all mauves and flimsiness. I don't feel that my nerves need all this soothing. In my case, for instance, I think the red and the strong moon shapes of 'Bishop of Llandaff' dahlias would add excellent spice to these kinds of flowers; or something greeny yellow, like *Patrinia scabiosifolia*, or orange, like *Asclepia tuberose*.

How much 'bite', how much 'spice' we want in our borders is, of course, a personal decision, and we must follow our own taste. The worst thing is to follow the prevalent 'good' taste promoted by fashionable magazines and television programmes, and timidly do what everyone else does – which all too often is to fill their borders with muted colours and grey plants. Remember Horace Walpole's comment in a letter, 'One of the greatest geniuses that ever existed, Shakespeare, undoubtedly wanted taste.' Surely it is better to attempt to be a horticultural Shakespeare than be frightened into subservience to the taste of the contemporary majority. John Betjeman, passionately defending his love of Victorian and Edwardian buildings in an age that derided them, called his first volume of architectural criticism *Ghastly Good Taste*. He was right: good taste can become tyrannical and result in uniform, predictable, ghastly gardens. To encourage us garden makers to be daring in doing what pleases us we should bear in mind a sentence from Boris Pasternak's *Dr Zhivago*: 'The calamity of mediocre taste is worse than the calamity of tastelessness.' The final word on this matter was said in the late nineteenth century by John Sedding: 'As to "codes of taste" (which are usually in matters of Art only someone's opinions stated pompously), these should not be allowed to baulk individual enterprise.'

ooooo

So how do you, a budding garden critic or a first-time garden maker, decide what is your taste? By looking at as wide a variety of gardens as possible, and asking yourself what it is you like about this combination of colours or shapes, and what you dislike about that one; why does this garden layout please you, this other not. Try to find the principle behind your objection or liking, so that in your own garden you do not merely avoid the hated object or merely copy the thing you like. And listen to the wise words of Marion Cran: 'Taste is not always a natural gift; but it can be acquired . . . The first thing to realize is that space, dignity and perspective are essential to a tasteful garden. Taste means controlled choosing, elimination, self-discipline.' This is why, as she explains, the flower lover, and even worse the flower collector, often makes an aesthetically poor garden; they are left exclaiming, 'It is such a mess; it never seems to mean anything.'

And Graham Stuart Thomas is on hand again with hints to get us started: 'It is my belief that so long as none of the red shades with blue in their composition are used with those which contain yellow, no clashes will occur. This seems to me to be a basic fact, but it eludes many people, especially those who have not thought about it, and do not understand their preferences.' Where do we draw the line between what Christopher Lloyd called 'spice' and a 'clash'? A 'clash' will jar our aesthetic sense; 'spice' will surprise and then, perhaps, delight. There will always be colours we like more than we like others. Many find yellow a colour difficult to handle in a border, and, as a result, corral all the yellows into a single border, or exclude the colour totally. At this point it is important to distinguish between colours and tones. Some yellows, for example, are stridently vivid, *Eschscholzia* for example, while others are more muted, like the evening primrose (*Oenothera*). Bright tones have their purpose as accents in a planting scheme, and the designer may use them to change the apparent proportions of a space, for they seem to advance towards the viewer. The garden critic should be aware of the reasons for using the tones that are chosen.

Some think that muted colours best suit the damp air of the British maritime climate, but global warming may put paid to the soft, misty light that our well-watered isle so often provides. Christopher Lloyd had only limited time for muted tones. His famous Long Border at Great Dixter challenges dreary, conventional good taste with strong colours in bold combinations, though it should be noted that the tones of the colours he uses are rarely strident. Take an example: he pairs *Inula magnifica* with the rose 'Florence May Morse', a bold red with a bold yellow, but neither colour is hard or 'jazzy' in tone. Is this kind of combination to your taste? If so, you will have many critics (not perceptive garden critics, but fault-finders) and must have the courage of your convictions. Lloyd said: 'I haven't got the inhibitions about colours that most people do – I like all the colours – but I wouldn't plant a pink 'Zépherin Drouhin' rose next to a scarlet *Lychnis chalcedonica*; there are limits.' It is these personal limits that the garden critic and the garden maker must establish for him or herself.

Some gardeners, perhaps to avoid charges of poor taste, like to gather together in a border flowers of the same colour. There is famous precedent for this in the red borders at Hidcote, although some of the reds tend towards purple and some have a hint of orange, and in the White Garden at Sissinghurst, which Vita Sackville-West thought of as a moonlight garden. Graham Stuart Thomas considered a white border the easiest to achieve; he went so far as to write, 'You can hardly go wrong with a white border.' I wonder how many white borders he had seen where little thought had been given to the shape of the plantings and the structural qualities of individual plants. Gertrude Jekyll had doubts about single-colour borders; she preferred to blend colours harmoniously. She wrote of a blue garden that it would be infinitely improved and brought to life with a touch of white or lemon yellow, 'but it is not allowed to have it because it is called the blue garden. I can see no sense in this; it seems to me like fetters foolishly self-imposed. Surely the business of the blue garden is to be beautiful as well as to be blue.' As we noted earlier, some colours, or rather the brightest tones of these colours, make such an impact that they seem to advance towards you and thus a border of bright yellows or whites will change the apparent shape of the space they define. Blue, as Mary Keen writes, 'is the colour for distance', so a blue border will seem to retreat into the haze of remoteness. This is because there are few strong, pure blues. A rare example is that extraordinary plant the sky-blue *Tweedia caerulea*; the first time I saw this flower I could not imagine it was real, so clear and pure the tone of the blue.

The great thing is not to be worried about violating some of the canons of current good taste; worry, and even worse anxiety, never makes a good garden. Good artists are not for ever looking over their shoulders to see if others approve. Listen, too, to the soothing words of one of England's great gardeners, Beth Chatto:

> If I am asked to pontificate about colour I always feel a bit stumped because I don't really set out with a colour scheme in mind. I am much more concerned with shapes, selecting first plants that are adapted to the conditions, with interesting foliage, which will furnish the scene for as long as possible. Then I pay attention to their flowers and add more ephemeral colour with bulbs, herbaceous plants, even half-hardies, to reinforce, or repeat colours. But after that, I am often excited by chance seedlings which may inject a colour I would not have thought of using.

A Christopher Lloyd border at Great Dixter, East Sussex, England

This acceptance of what happens by chance is surely the sign of the relaxed and true gardener, who adapts to the flow of nature – not always but sometimes. A garden that just follows the designer's planting plan will look stiff and awkward and will lack the *sine qua non* of a really good garden – atmosphere.

The Dublin gardener Helen Dillon, writing to Christopher Lloyd after visiting Great Dixter, complimented him on his borders having 'great presence', but found it hard to explain what was so good about them: 'no question of waffling along in subtle colour schemes – perhaps it's that you are more aware of shape than most gardeners.' This is a factor in garden composition that is much less discussed than colour, as if plants were only colours, not also pieces of living sculpture. Some great designers, like Roberto Burle Marx, began life as painters, and his practice was to paint his designs before laying them out on the ground. For him plants were colours on a palette. Getrude Jekyll, too, insisted that gardeners should think like painters: 'in setting a garden we are painting a picture . . . so that to paint it rightly is a debt we owe to the beauty of the flowers and the light of the sun . . . the colours should be placed with careful forethought and deliberation, as a painter employs them on his picture, and not dropped down in lifeless dabs.' And such is the influence of Jekyll that her concern with colour has blinded many to the importance of the shapes of plants and planting. In some of the great borders all the taller plants are grouped at the back with the shorter in front, so that we see ascending layers of colour. But if some taller plants are given a front seat in the border, they will enclose small areas, like miniature theatres, in which dramatic incidents of colour combination can be partially isolated from the rest of the planting. The disadvantage of such an arrangement is that such tall plants at the front will interrupt the view along the border from the side.

Individual plants have shape in their leaves as well as structural form and colour in their flowers. A story told by Joe Eck, the American designer, underlines this point:

> A great English plantsman was once called in to evaluate a perennial garden which, for reasons mysterious to the owner, was vaguely displeasing to her. She had taken care to secure the best plants and had attended scrupulously to color harmonies. Maintenance was just as it should be. Still, the composition failed to satisfy. After strolling round the garden, admiring the fine plants there and the horticultural skill that had brought them to perfection, the plantsman's verdict was swift and sure. 'Your leaves are all the same size.'

Many plants are floppy, even to the point of needing a crutch to keep them upright, but some have a marked upright posture. *Echinops ritro* is an example. Grasses, which are so fashionable at the moment, have a distinctive shape, and as a result are often best planted as single specimens, not in messy borders of grasses, where they collapse on top of each other. When they are combined with other grasses, or packed tightly into a mixed border, the shape of their fountaining wands is less easily appreciated.

Arranging the plants for colour combinations and for their harmony of shape is perhaps not the most important thing to think about if we are place making, rather than merely decorating the ground. Mary Keen in *Gardens of Inspiration* reminds us that 'Flowers are the outward trappings, and I think they can mar as well as make a garden. If they fight the spirit of the place, as so often they do, then everything else is wasted. The real point is the place and what it does to you as a person.' It is good to be reminded that flowers are not always the most important thing in a garden, particularly if one is English and has imbibed from birth the doctrine that a garden is a place for flowers and a lawn; the Oriental gardener and the gardener from the Islamic world scarcely have need of Keen's admonition. A final warning on flowers and colour comes from Russell Page: 'when there is a distant view, carelessly used colour will destroy the whole meaning of the garden. Consciously or unconsciously, both eye and mind will shift from flowers to view and back again, and find no rest.' Yes, flowers and their colours can be a distraction.

Let us conclude this section on taste by returning to the eighteenth century, the period in which the word was so prominent, and, interestingly, the period in which garden visiting became a fashionable pastime. It was an age that took both taste and gardening more seriously than we do. Thus Horace Walpole in 1770 could write: 'Poetry, Painting and Gardening . . . will, forever, by men of taste be deemed three sisters, or the three new Graces who dress and adorn nature.' Who today would rank gardening as one of the fine arts? Hume's essay *Of the Standard of Taste* (1757) still has much to teach critics of all kinds, including garden critics whose taste will be apparent in their judgments and garden makers whose taste will be revealed in their creations. Hume warns us against the prejudice of the closed mind as 'destructive of sound judgment', and against complacency: 'We are apt to call barbarous whatever departs widely from our own taste and apprehension; but soon find the epithet of reproach retorted on us.' He emphasizes that beauty is subjective: 'Beauty is no quality in things themselves; it exists merely in the mind which perceives them; and each mind perceives a different beauty.' But he also insists that experience in looking at beautiful things, and particularly in comparing them, is a necessary qualification for a critic if he or she is to form sound, persuasive judgments. His conclusion is that critics have a valuable role to play but they must prepare themselves carefully, so that their taste is sound: 'Strong sense, united to delicate sentiment [a modern writer would use the word 'sensitivity'], improved by practice, perfected by comparison, and cleared of all prejudice, can alone entitle critics to this valuable character' – that is, to be called critics. And such preparation can only be done by looking at the gardens we are visiting or the gardens we are making more attentively, by experiencing them more completely.

6 STYLE AND MEANING

'Style is a matter of taste; design is a matter of principle.'

Thomas Church

'The Garden, to put it portentously, is an epiphany of man's relationship to mystery. This relationship is its meaning.'

David E. Cooper

When we talk about an artist's style, we are discussing the way he or she uses the medium of that particular art – words for the writer, paint and sounds for the painter and musician; the style of a garden lies in the way plants, water, hard landscaping and so on are used. Perhaps Russell Page expressed most clearly in *The Education of a Gardener* what garden makers are doing when they decide on a style that suits their taste and is appropriate to the place they are making: 'Style for the garden designer means to assemble all the physical elements of a garden scene, to blend them into a coherent whole and to imbue the whole with all the intensity, or, perhaps I should say, "intelligence" that he can muster, so that the whole may have a quality peculiar to itself.' The chosen style will derive from the purpose or idea (often, for the professional designer, an expression of the wishes of the client) that lies behind the whole garden, which guides the garden maker in deciding what to include and what to reject, and in how to treat the site. If the style is coherently thought out and executed, then the garden will feel peaceful and at ease. As the designer and teacher John Brookes has written: 'Style is not about seeing how many differing plants you can cram in; it's about achieving visual tranquillity.' Page argues that style cannot be other than contemporary; even if we borrow ideas from a previous age or another country, he claims, we will interpret those ideas in a way that is contemporary and local.

And where is this guiding idea that determines the style to come from? It may be from the imagination of the garden maker, so that the garden is a kind of personal fantasy, unrelated to the place where it is created or to the cultural history of the country where it exists. An example of this kind of garden is the remarkable Sacro Bosco made by Pier Francesco Orsini not far from Viterbo, north of Rome. This is a sixteenth-century garden but shows nothing of the swaggering style, with theatrical steps and formal terraces, that prevailed in the Papal States at the time. Orsini placed an inscription near the entrance to his sacred grove which, teasingly, asks the visitor to consider every detail of his creation, all the monstrous sculptures and provocative inscriptions, and then 'tell me whether you think it is made as a trick or as a work of art'. A more modern example of a fantasy garden is the Giardino dei Tarocchi (the Garden of the Tarot Cards), a little further north in Italy, on the borders of Lazio and Tuscany. Here between 1979 and 1996 Niki de Saint Phalle created a wildly imaginative collection of huge figures from the Tarot pack, built in reinforced concrete; they are covered in mosaics of ceramic and mirror, so that they are not only colourful

Left and right Giardino dei Tarocchi, Capalbio, Italy

but flash in the sunlight. The figures are so huge that you can climb inside them and upon them. These two creations are extreme examples of gardens that sprang from their creators' unshackled imaginations. But more modest gardens, also, will to some extent reflect the dreams and desires of their makers.

Often the guiding idea for a garden's style will spring from the architecture of the house, and this will determine how the garden is to look, at least in the immediate surroundings of the buildings. It is significant that neither the Sacro Bosco nor the Giardino dei Tarocchi are related to any house; their isolation from a human dwelling place gave freer rein to their creators' imaginations. The house itself may, of course, be the product of someone's fantasy. In the heart of rural England we can find a wonderful architectural anomaly: the house at Sezincote which Sir Charles Cockerell had built by his architect brother in the early nineteenth century. The onion domes and chattris of Moghul architecture are not something we expect to find in the gentle countryside of the Cotswold hills. All becomes clearer when we learn that the Cockerell family had had a long association with the East India Company. And what kind of garden would suit

Sezincote, Moreton-in-Marsh, England

such a house? Repton was consulted but it is unclear how many of his ideas were put into practice. The Moghul style of the house was continued in the grounds, where an Indian-style bridge, with a fine pair of Brahma bulls at each end, crosses the stream, and there is even a temple to Surya, the sun goddess, designed by Thomas Daniell. But perhaps the most memorable part of the gardens at Sezincote is the Paradise Garden, which lies close to the house; this mid-twentieth-century addition was designed to imitate classical Moghul gardens, with canals crossing at right angles and Irish yews taking the place of cypresses, the trees of eternity. In 1965 Lady Kleinwort returned from India and decided to take the neglected garden in hand; since this part lay so close to the house, she and her designer, Graham Stuart Thomas, wisely decided to echo the Moghul style that was already the predominant feature of the architecture.

If you had deep pockets, as the Egerton family at Tatton Park in Cheshire did, then you might have as many styles as you liked, and in your spacious acres there would be no danger that one would clash with another. In the late eighteenth century the ubiquitous Humphry Repton was called in, but his advice to turn the beech avenue into clumps of trees was not followed. Later the family decided to have an Italian garden, when that was the fashion in the mid-nineteenth century, and theirs was designed by the eminent Joseph Paxton. Its terraces, balustrades, steps, urns and fountains have been recently restored to their full glory, and adorned with some eye-popping bedding, which might well have suited mid-Victorian taste, but today is seen mainly in municipal parks. Sixty years later another garden style came into vogue, and, after a visit to the Japanese exhibition at White City in 1910, Alan de Tatton decided he must have a Japanese garden. Workers were imported from Japan and a version of the tea garden, complete with Shinto temple, was created on an island site. A perhaps apocryphal story is told of this, and of several other Japanese gardens created at this period: a visiting Japanese dignitary comments with ambiguous tact: 'We have nothing like this in our country.' But authenticity was not the point, any more than it had been at Biddulph Grange in Staffordshire, where James Bateman had brought together an Egyptian garden with sphinxes, a Chinese garden with scarlet painted bridges and a Staffordshire cottage. The mixture of styles tells us much about the Victorians' global ambitions and interests, though some have claimed that this ambition results in tasteless confusion.

But why decide to imitate a foreign style in an English country garden? The motives may be found in the biography of the creator, as in the close connections

The Japanese Garden,
Tatton Park, Knutsford,
England

between the Cockerell family and India. But individual lives do not always explain the roots of a taste for the exotic. Fashion, either universal or national, for a particular foreign style may be the explanation, and this is certainly easier for the historian to detect and explain. The Italian Garden at Tatton Park is part of the wave of formal gardens that began to sweep England in the early nineteenth century as the dialectic of fashion swung away from 'Capability' Brown's acres of grass, clumps of trees and 'natural' landscaping towards something more obviously artificial. At Tatton Park the house, remodelled in the early years of the nineteenth century by Lewis Wyatt, needed a more stately setting. And the Japanese Garden? The taste for all things Japanese in late nineteenth-century Europe can be seen, for example, in the paintings of Monet and, indeed, in his house at Giverny; it sprang from the opening up of Japan to the outside world, after it had been closed in defiant isolation, by order of the Shogun, for more than two hundred years. In 1893 there was a Japanese presence at the World's Columbia Exhibition in Chicago, and trade with Japan was developing; increasing contacts between Europe and Japan meant that cultural influences were soon passing in both directions.

So the style of a garden may be decided by the prevailing fashion, by the architecture of the house or by the whimsical dream of the creator, but it may also be guided by the site of the garden itself. When Italian princes of the church began to build their country villas around Rome in the sixteenth century, they followed the advice of Leon Battista Alberti and sited them on hills, where the air was better and the views more extensive. This meant that their gardens had to occupy the slopes above and below the house, which could only happen if the hillside was terraced, following agricultural practice. Thus was born the style of garden we think of as Italian with ornate steps, balustrades and straight walks. If water was available, as it is in abundance at the Villa d'Este in Tivoli, then you could have fountains and water games to cool the air and the visitors. Shade was necessary, so pergolas were built and cypresses planted. In deserts, too, the site dictated what the garden should be: a kind of paradise containing all that the desert lacked, flowing with water, shaded by trees producing fruit in abundance and bejewelled with flowers. Usually gardens of this Islamic/Persian tradition are walled (our word 'paradise' derives from the Persian word meaning 'walled around'); thus they turn their backs on their setting, so as to concentrate on fulfilling the escapist dreams of their creators. Contained gardens such as these, and the Oriental gardens of China and Japan, are often the same, having an intense style of their own, which takes the Western visitor far away from Christian Europe and demands an understanding of a culture quite unfamiliar to many of us.

It may be that the English garden maker will choose something more home-grown as the dominant influence in his or her garden – the cottage garden style, for example. This has a particular appeal not only for patriotic and nostalgic reasons, but also because it seems to suit the smaller gardens that most of us now have. What is this style that has enchanted us in the paintings of Helen Allingham and Kate Greenaway? Their gardens, crammed full of flourishing plants tended by rosy-cheeked figures in bonnets and spotless aprons, are, of course, a romantic fiction. The real cottage garden was used to produce food for the family, and where there was space available a random assortment of flowers was wedged in among the vegetables. Often these plants had come from neighbours, or they were spares from the flower garden of the 'great house', passed on by an obliging gardener or gardener's boy. Thus cottage gardens provided a refuge for a wide range of unfashionable herbaceous plants when all the rage at the 'great house' was for floral bedding; this is one reason these gardens were so highly prized by Gertrude Jekyll and William Robinson. But in our gardens do we want our carefully selected specimens to be shoved in wherever there is room, and to be mixed up with the vegetables in our borders? Perhaps we might allow in some red-leaved beet – but only because it fits our colour scheme. Our kind of cottage gardening is different; there is, as Vita Sackville-West wrote, 'a pleasing touch of Marie Antoinette-ism about it. For while the method is that of the cottage gardener, the material is more sophisticated.' We want the relaxed opulence and romantic 'naturalness' of the fictional cottage garden, but not the mud and poverty that used to go with the real thing.

Of course, the visiting garden critic will not expect to find an exact reproduction of any one style, native or imported (remember Russell Page's dictum that a garden should have 'a quality peculiar to itself'), but perhaps to detect its influence on the way the garden has been made. The delight will lie in the way the garden is personal and idiosyncratic, in the way it plays variations on an established, traditional style. The courtyard garden at Mapperton in Dorset sets off the sixteenth-century house ideally, but there is a surprise waiting for the visitor hidden in a deep valley. Here the garden maker was free to follow any style because the site is distant and hidden from the house by the steepness of the hills that enclose the valley, while on the opposite hill there are only open fields.

What might we expect to find in this rustic setting? Certainly not a formal, Italian garden, complete with pools, fountains, stone steps, yew buttresses and statuary. The effect is breathtaking because it is so daring and impossible to predict. Here is an imitation of a well-established and familiar garden style but, when found in an enclosed, rural setting, its formality strikes us anew, and makes us rethink how this style can be used. Such a rectilinear layout does not often make us feel we have entered a wonderland, but here at Mapperton it makes a powerful appeal to the visitor's imagination.

Many gardens have a part that is more formal in style and a part that is less formal; the transition from one to the other will be better or worse handled, and the proportion of one to the other will tell us of the taste of the garden maker. At the turn of the twentieth century there was an absurd battle between supporters of the formal style and those who supported the informal; two doughty champions emerged, both of them eloquent writers, to represent either view, Reginald Blomfield in the formal corner and William Robinson defending a more 'natural' style of gardening. Blomfield explained the object of formal gardening, which is 'to make the house grow out of its surroundings, and to prevent its being an excrescence on the face of nature. The building cannot resemble anything in nature, unless you are content with a mud-hut and cover it with grass.' Following his advice, many gardeners choose to have a formal area close to the house, while further away architectural straight lines give way to the curves and informal, though carefully thought out, planting that Robinson championed.

And what if the garden maker wants a style more contemporary, less retrospective? Is there such a thing as a contemporary, twenty-first-century garden style? Perhaps the most striking element in a self-consciously modern garden is its uncluttered look, using clean, bold lines, sparse planting with shrubs of dramatic form such as yuccas, and modern materials like dyed concrete, steel and plastic. The colours, too, will be bold, often in large blocks, as in a Mondrian painting. Or, perhaps even more up to the minute, the style may be that of a 'conceptual garden', which, as its name suggests, is a garden where a single idea is dominant. In such gardens artifice is celebrated and no attempt is made to conceal human intervention; as Tim Richardson explains: 'The role of the artist is paramount, while the old idea of nature as a legitimate guiding force is rejected.' Out with the old, in with the new; though, as we shall see, the conceptual garden is not such a new idea after all. Richardson is explicit: 'Conceptualist landscape design is predicated on the idea of meaning, metaphor or narrative', so there may be little room for beauty and, sometimes, a visitor must work hard to detect what the garden is saying. The critic may perhaps ask what such a garden is like to be in, not just to look at, perhaps in photographs; as Louisa Jones asks, 'Do you feel welcome? Invited, excluded, overwhelmed, underwhelmed?'; or you may feel in need of an explanation – a guide or a guidebook. Often photographs make gardens of this type look elegantly simple, even beautiful, at the very least, challenging to the intellect, but they do not tell us what it is like being in, for example, The Garden of Cosmic Speculation near Dumfries created by Charles Jencks and the late Maggie Keswick.

Metaphor and narrative are to be found, though never at the expense of beauty, in many of the great High Renaissance Italian gardens with their iconographical 'programmes'; these an educated, contemporary visitor would have been able to elucidate, at least in part. For example, the garden at the Villa d'Este in Tivoli with its coats of arms including the heraldic white eagle was clearly intended to vaunt the glory of Ippolito d'Este's family. But, less obviously, the references to Hercules in various parts of the garden would have been understood only by those who knew that the d'Este family claimed descent from this hero. And that is not the only story that lies behind the garden's design. As you descend the steps from the house you may turn right or left along the first great terrace; turning right takes you to the Oval Fountain and the representation of the town of Tivoli; turn left and you will reach the Rometta, a miniaturization of some of the great sights in Rome. A dialogue begins here between the pleasures of the country town and the glories of Rome, and between nature and art. Sadly, much of the statuary was removed from the garden in the eighteenth century, so that many clues to the garden's meaning are now irretrievably lost. At the Villa Lante in Bagnaia there is an equally intricate 'programme', though it is made harder to read because today's visitor enters the garden from the 'wrong' end. Cardinal Gambara's sixteenth-century guests would have entered the garden at the top, through the wood. On the top terrace they would have first encountered rustic stonework and the water gushing from rough, moss-covered spouts; this is the beginning of the story of water that the garden tells. As visitors descend the hillside they find references to the destructive power of water in Deucalion's flood, but slowly the element is tamed, until, docile, it runs along the middle of the Cardinal's *al fresco* dining table. The river gods Tiber and Arno make a majestic appearance, bearing their cornucopia signifying the abundance that tamed water guarantees. And finally, escaping from the shade of the garden, water lies still in the bright sunshine of the square, symmetrically patterned parterre on the lowest terrace.

The twenty-first century visitor will, perhaps, fail to appreciate the theme that the Villa Lante garden is illustrating, though an educated sixteenth-century visitor, schooled in searching artworks for their political, moral and mythological significance, would have understood it. But today's visitor will still enjoy the beautiful proportions of the garden, the rushing water, the contrasts of light and shade, the lichen-covered stonework, the majestic plane trees. Does it matter that, as T.S. Eliot put it, 'we had the experience but missed the meaning'? From time to time the question 'what matters more in a garden, its meaning or its beauty?' comes to the surface (for some contemporary contributions to this debate, see the stimulating website thinkingardens.com), and it is no surprise to find that in the eighteenth century, as England moved towards a more romantic type of gardening, English voices were heard deploring the metaphorical

The Dining Table, Villa Lante, Bagnaia, Italy

'readings' that some earlier gardens demanded. One of the most influential was Thomas Whately. His anonymously published *Observations on Modern Gardening* (1770) was widely read not only in England but in Europe, as it was rapidly translated into both French and German. He objected to what he called 'emblematic' gardens and their decorations that required interpretation: referring to the statues and carved inscriptions so common in earlier gardens, he writes, 'All these devices are rather emblematical than expressive . . . they make no immediate impression, for they must be examined, compared, perhaps explained, before the whole design of them is well understood.' From the Romantic age onwards there has been much less discussion of a garden's appeal to the intellect, and thus less reference to the meanings that gardens convey.

The styles of Oriental and Islamic gardens contain meanings that are sometimes difficult for the Westerner to elucidate, and, certainly in the Oriental culture, an important part of their beauty lies in the suggestions and literary references to be adduced from the garden's composition. In Moghul tomb gardens, for example, the octagonal water bowls signify the blend of the eternal, the circle, with the human and impermanent, the square – the unspoken hope being that the one who has died has moved on to a more permanent world. Different cultures will also look for different things in their gardens: the Chinese, for example, love twisted rocks piled up, because in them they see an expression of the energy of nature, the 'ch'i'. More than this, the holes in these pitted rocks are the 'yin' and 'yang' of voids contrasting with solidity, and as the sun moves during the day, the shadows on the face of the pitted stone are always changing its appearance. Then again the rock piles suggest, although in miniature, mountains, where dwell the sages and the gods; usually the visitor ascends these miniature hills along twisting paths that enforce a slow, meditative pace. Westerners may not judge the rock piles to be beautiful but that is to miss their point. Sometimes the meaning the garden expresses lies too deep for words, so deeply embedded is its understanding in the culture of the country; the Japanese phrase *wabi sabi*, often used of the beauty to be found in something worn and old, is almost impossible to translate, or even explain fully, though every Japanese understands the phrase instantly and completely. Individual plants, too, have significance in Oriental gardens; the bamboo for instance with its hollow stem signifies the person who has little pride and can bend when circumstances turn difficult, yet retains a certain resilience and will not easily break. If, however, we Westerners can only laboriously translate each element of an Oriental garden into a meaning we can understand, we necessarily miss the delicately allusive experience that the garden as a whole offers.

These Oriental gardens allude not only to the ch'i of Tao'ist philosophy, and to Confucian teachings on individual conduct as exemplified by the bamboo, but also contain references to the long traditions of painting and literature in the Middle Kingdom. Garden views were often set up to imitate famous scroll paintings, and in gardens we find references, sometimes verbal and explicit, sometimes implicit, to ancient folk tales; for example, to the story of Peach Blossom Spring, in which a fisherman loses his way in a series of caves and finds himself in a country of ideal, unfading beauty. On his return to the everyday world he can, of course, never find his way back to this perfect land, but neither can he stop dreaming of it. Here we find represented the escape from the real world that all gardens of all traditions and styles to some extent offer us; they are dream places. Such an escape can be a trap, of course, as in Giorgio Bassani's great novel *The Garden of the Finzi Contini*, in which the Jewish family found it all too easy to dream away their lives, playing tennis in their beautiful garden, and ignore the rising tide of anti-Semitism that was sweeping early twentieth-century Italy.

Rock work beautifully framed at the Dr Sun Yat-Sen Garden, Vancouver, Canada

It is easy for an outsider coming to the gardens of an alien tradition with a closed mind (see Chapter 3) to misjudge them; 'Where are the flowers?' the horrified Anglo-Saxon exclaims. When we travel, it is difficult not to take with us the cultural assumptions about garden style our education has implanted in us. Sir John Chardin, writing of Persian gardens in 1686, commented that while the native flora is very rich, few of these beautiful plants are used in their gardens. He complains also that Persian gardens are flat and laid out in formal straight lines, regretting, 'They don't know what Parterres and Greenhouses, what Wildernesses and Terraces, and other ornaments of our gardens are.' Chardin put this down to the fact that the lazy Oriental seldom walks in his garden; he merely sits and enjoys the cool air and the sound of the fountains. It is important that the garden visitor identifies the style of the garden being visited; we cannot, for example, expect a garden dedicated to the well-being of its wildlife to have the same kind of trim, finished quality we expect of a traditional English flower garden.

And if we mistake the kind of garden we may, equally, mistake the meaning it is trying to convey. Some gardens are made to be inhabited and some to be looked at; many are both. Japanese gardens are often to be looked at from a pre-determined point of view; they are pictorial compositions that would sometimes be spoiled if a human figure intruded into their carefully crafted false perspective. Chinese gardens, however, are to be inhabited but also contain precisely arranged views, often to be seen from the windows of the pavilions, which focus the visitor's attention on what is to be looked at; in the Yu Yuan garden in Shanghai, for example, the Jade Grace Pavilion provides a place where the visitor can sit and admire the Exquisitely Carved Jade Stone, a particularly fine T'ai Hu rock.

On a visit to the United States, the foreign visitor may be disturbed by the lack of boundaries to the gardens, a feature typical of the American garden style, at least on the east coast. In the suburbs the great American lawn flows on from one house to another with no break, and no apparent indication of where one property ends and the next begins. In these gardens there is little to distinguish one garden from another, no expression of personality or taste, in fact a total lack of style. To criticize this is to misunderstand the function of this uniformity. In a country of immigrants coming from places with quite different garden styles, this imposed lack of self-expression has a social function; 'We're all Americans now,' it says. And the weekly mowing of your section of the communal lawn becomes a rite that helps bind the community together in a common endeavour to keep the street looking tidy. In American country gardens the lack of a boundary has something to say about the relationship between the householders and the wilderness, with its powerful, mythic hold on the American imagination. Again if we criticize the style of these gardens without understanding we shall judge them wrongly.

When we know more of the Oriental and Islamic traditions, we can understand their gardens better, but this understanding remains something we have learned; it does not form part of our experience of the garden, as it would for someone native to those traditions. We translate, if we can, an alien form of poetic understanding into terms that make them comprehensible to us, but still the understanding is too narrow, too cerebral. As David Cooper has written, when discussing the meaning of gardens, 'An arrangement of rocks may depict one thing, allude to another, express a certain attitude, be symptomatic of its times, and have personal associations for the gardener.' And all these things may be called layers of 'meaning' to be found in just one element of a garden's composition, which shows how complex is the discussion of meaning when any kind of garden art is our subject.

Gardens are often discussed in terms of architecture – the division and proportions of space, for example – and of painting – the harmony of colours and the skill of the composition. But when we think of their meanings, I wonder if we should not think of gardens more in terms of music. Wolfgang Hildesheimer in his book on Mozart talks of music as 'an important medium of information. But the information . . . escapes both analysis and calculation, because it conveys no semantic meaning. It cannot be translated into words, but exists and functions parallel to them, as a supplementary and fully-fledged means of expression.' He goes on to say that music is a stimulus that 'mobilizes feelings that are reserved exclusively for it, and is assimilated according to the receptivity of the listener'. Maybe these feelings that are mobilized by music and similar feelings aroused by a garden are the reason that both these arts have the therapeutic benefits that are being increasingly understood, and move us in ways that seem to be beyond words and deeply spiritual. Perhaps Walter Pater was right when he wrote that 'All art constantly aspires to the condition of music.'

Like pieces of music, gardens sometimes use words, the more everyday medium of communication, to convey their meanings, or at the least to stimulate cerebral cogitation. For years the naming of places and pavilions in Chinese gardens has been of great importance; for example, a building is called the

Pavilion for Enjoying the Scent that Comes from Afar, and there the visitor is asked to focus on the impressions experienced by a sense other than the eye. In the eighteenth-century Chinese novel *The Story of the Stone* a newly made garden, which is eventually named Prospect Garden, is visited by its owner, Jia Zheng, and his unpromising son Bao-yu, and the latter is charged with naming some of the features of the garden. To his father's surprise he does so in elegant couplets, which in their turn make reference to some of the most famous poems of Chinese literature. Thus gardening takes its place in the artistic life and cultural traditions of the country. In mid-eighteenth-century England William Shenstone decorated his farm walk at The Leasowes with inscriptions to draw attention to the beauties of particular views. Many of these were quotations from Virgil, but some he wrote himself, not always to happy effect: 'Here in cool grot, and mossy cell,/We rural fays and faeries dwell' was intended to work on the visitor's imagination, I suppose. Ian Hamilton Finlay, the concrete poet, used words in gardens more allusively and wittily. For example, in the Improvement Garden

Ian Hamilton Finlay's herd of sheep at Stockwood Park, Luton, England

he designed for Stockwood Park in Luton a curved wall with beautifully carved inscriptions is titled 'Errata of Ovid'; the words ask the reader to think of the natural objects rather than the humans before their metamorphosis; thus 'For Daphne read Laurel' and 'For Philomela read Nightingale', and, provocatively, 'For Narcissus read Narcissus'. Unlike gardens whose meanings come to us indirectly and obliquely, gardens with words stimulate us to think in ways we are used to, but sometimes they also cause us to rethink our experience of being in a garden.

The words that Sheppard Craige uses at Il Bosco della Ragnaia in Tuscany, and the way they are used, help to point up the meaning of the place he is making – which is no less than a contemporary *sacro bosco*, or sacred grove, but far different from Orsini's creation at Bomarzo. The wood where he is working has been thinned and some plants have been added. There has also been some working of the ground, but all the changes have been done in such a tactful way that the atmosphere of the wood is intact. Its mysterious shades, the processional avenue along which we approach the wood, and the way we descend into it from the sunny hillside, all add to the sense of mystery and ceremony – and each has been shaped by Craige in his own style, which, in turn, is dictated by the experience or meaning at which he is aiming. Much is left to chance and the forces of nature; fallen leaves are allowed to decay where they fall, and any wild flowers that can bear the gloom are welcomed. Water has been added in still pools and, less successfully, in a water chute. But while visitors will undoubtedly respond to the atmosphere of the wood, to experience the place more fully they need words – words that hint at a meaning but do not define it. An example: we find a cabinet containing balances and levels; then, not far away we see a circular pool with a circular stone in the middle on which are inscribed the words 'Aequus Animus', meaning 'balanced mind or spirit'. We are not being preached at or hectored but gently nudged towards an understanding of the power of the place, which often raises questions in the mind of the visitor, rather than teaching lessons – or, perhaps, the questions are the lesson. Thus we find the Altar of Skepticism (sic: Craige is American), inscribed with the question Montaigne addressed to himself: '*Que sais je?*' More than many other made places (it does not seem appropriate to call it a garden), this one invites a dialogue with the visitor, and the way words are used is an essential part of the place's style, meaning and atmosphere.

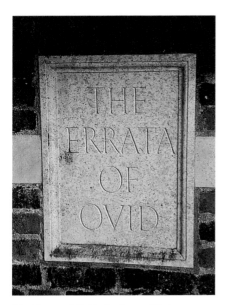

The Errata of Ovid, Stockwood Park, Luton, England

The usual choice of style a designer offers the client who knows nothing about gardens is that between formal and informal, but this is to miss the main point about a garden: its atmosphere, its appeal to the imagination, the special quality of that particular 'place'. The question the designer should ask is: 'What do you want from your garden?' The garden's style will flow from the answer to that question – see Chapter 1. A garden's style can provide a lively stimulus to visitors' imaginations, transporting them out of their real historical or geographical setting. The sight of a rigidly formal garden with symmetrical yew hedges and grass banks, like the Tiltyard at Dartington Hall in Devon, may conjure up visions of knights in armour at a jousting tournament; an Italianate garden with elegantly proportioned steps and balustrades may evoke memories of High Renaissance villas in the Roman *campagna* – though in Britain the effect may be somewhat spoiled by the misty English light. A visit to an Oriental or Islamic garden will carry us far from Christian Europe. And the garden critic will want to know why the garden has been made in this style. Is it to echo the architecture of the house, like the so-called Moghul garden at Sezincote, or just to serve the whim of the maker? '*Le style est l'homme même*,' said Buffon, and, if he is right, then in 'reading' the garden and its meaning we shall also find evidence of the personality of its maker.

In conclusion we might return to Russell Page and the questions he suggests we ask when searching for a style around which to build the garden we are making:

> Do you want to grow your own flowers and vegetables, make a collection of plants or specialize in one or another form of horticulture? Does your garden represent just so much more living-space for the pool, outdoor dining-room and children's playground? Do you want to create a pictorial composition

private to yourself, or do you want to draw in the landscape beyond the garden and use your plot to make a frame for the world outside? Whatever your choice or your need, it is such considerations that will determine your limitations and so establish a first foundation for style.

For the garden critic it will be useful to ask how the garden maker has answered these questions – what kind of a garden has she or he made, how memorable is the atmosphere, and what can we learn of the character of the maker from the creation we are visiting. The style of the garden, if a coherent style has been achieved, will lead us towards answers to all these questions.

Il Sacro Bosco, Bomarzo, Italy

7 MEMORY AND ATMOSPHERE

'Memory is a gardener's real palette; memory as it summons up the past, memory as it shapes the present, memory as it dictates the future.'

Jamaica Kincaid, *My Garden (Book)*

Gardens have a particularly intimate connection with memory, both folk memory and individual memory. Gardeners, for example, never forget the name of someone who has given them a plant – at least as long as the plant is alive. In the folk memory, fed by myths, children's stories and religion, the garden is the perfect place, which we may be allowed to enjoy for a time but from which we are later excluded, or of which we are given only a passing glimpse, perhaps in a dream. The garden, a shaped and cultivated place, contrasts with the wastes of the world. Adam and Eve, expelled from an Eden where, eternally infantile, all they had to do was obey, have to make their adult way in the trackless world of undefined, inchoate space; no wonder they move, in Milton's words, 'with wandering steps and slow'. A similar experience of an ideal place, now lost, seems often to haunt the individual memory, but here it is particularly gardens experienced in childhood, often grandmothers' gardens, and from these we are exiled by the natural process of development and by the experiences of adulthood – the complications of sex, ambition and so on. As children we could enjoy these gardens instinctively and uncritically, but adult life blurs the responses of the instincts while sharpening the critical intelligence. Wordsworth, with a belief in the almost mystical experience we enjoy in childhood that is typical of a romantic, perhaps understood: 'Sweet is the lore that Nature brings,/Our meddling intellect/Misshapes the beauteous forms of things:/We murder to dissect.'

Ninfa, Latina, Italy

Gardens experienced in adult life, too, may linger in the memory. Sometimes this happens because the moment of our visit was so idyllic – the light was falling at the perfect angle, the temperature was just right, birds were singing, scents were lingering in the air; it was a moment that seemed out of time, something given, like a revelation. Or it may be that the visitor had just fallen in love, eaten an exceptional lunch or had her first novel accepted, and the garden comes to meet such ecstatic individuals, seeming to echo their happiness so perfectly that the memory of the moment will never leave them. Gardens do not only respond to the mood of the visitor: they can also change that mood. We have already looked at the healing power of working in a garden and have made reference to the experience of the mourner who felt consoled by her visit to a garden. Why do such garden moments stay in our minds? Compare a garden remembered with a photograph of the same garden: what is the difference? Obviously the photograph cannot capture the sounds of birdsong and the wind in the trees, the warmth of the sun or the softness of the grass underfoot. But more importantly it cannot capture the experience of time – the cloud that blotted out the sun for an instant, the first petal seen falling from the blossoming rose, the sense that you, the visitor or the garden are at their peak, and that you have been allowed, just for a moment, to live more intensely than usual. Looking at the photograph clarifies this point. What makes a garden experience memorable is much more than what we take in with our eyes; the colour combinations in the border may be perfect, the lawn immaculately daisy free, but such things are not enough by themselves to lodge the experience in the memory.

So what is it that makes a garden memorable? To answer this question I want to consider two gardens which, at first glance, could scarcely seem more different yet both seem completely unforgettable in the totality of the experience they offer: Ninfa, south of Rome, with its soft, damp air, grass underfoot, ruins and rushing water; and the Wang Xi Yuan in Suzhou, China, a walled, town garden, with pebble paths, sparse planting and piles of pock-marked rock. Ninfa seems buried deep in the European memory and half familiar from myriad eighteenth-century paintings of the Roman *campagna*; the Wang Xi is completely unfamiliar to the Western eye, shockingly unlike any garden seen before – for a start it has few plants, while Ninfa is said to have more than 10,000 species. Then the Chinese garden has the tense excitement of a highly wrought, intricate work of art, while Ninfa has all the relaxation of a romantic garden, so that it almost persuades visitors that they have stumbled upon a work of nature, not of art. And finally there is the difference in size: the Wang Xi garden is little more than an acre/0.4 hectares, within which it manages to encompass ten small courtyard gardens, as well as many pavilions and halls. Ninfa, by contrast, is spread over more than 20 deep-breathing, relaxed acres/8 hectares.

So the Occidental visitor entering the Suzhou garden is at first baffled. It is impossible to know what to look at first; no symmetry guides the eye, and there are no views laid out with eye-catchers as their focal points. And which direction should we take? Moon gateways and narrow, hump-backed bridges seem equally inviting. At Ninfa a path shows us the way to go, and paths, as that extraordinary park maker Prince Hermann Pückler-Muskau wrote, are the silent guides to a garden. We will have taken scarcely a step or two in the Italian garden before we hear the sound of water rushing powerfully down to the river. There seems, in this first part of the garden, to be water everywhere; superabundant water, so that in one place a miniature aqueduct carries one stream over another. At the Wang Xi, by contrast, the main courtyard is built around a still, dark pool of irregular shape, in which the surrounding buildings are perfectly reflected; around its edge, seats are provided, their backs curving out over the water, so the visitor, twisting round, can look straight down into the dark depths and admire the frolicking fish.

How can it be that two such different gardens have an equally strong appeal and lodge themselves so completely in the memory? An answer might begin by noticing the way they are both decisively cut off from the mundane world of common experience; they are places apart, retreats from the ordinary, the stressful, the ugly. The name Wang Xi Yuan points to this atmosphere of otherworldliness; it translates as the Master of the Fishing Nets Garden, and fishing had a special significance in the world of the mandarin civil service. When British ministers of the Crown decide to retire or withdraw from government office, they often claim they want to spend more time with their families; the Chinese mandarin would say he wanted to spend more time fishing, by which he meant more time writing poetry, practising his calligraphy, drinking with friends, meditating and cultivating that serenity of mind the Buddha taught was the highest good. And both gardens offer this sense of a place apart with enormous intensity: the Wang Xi because every detail of paving, rockwork and planting is so perfect that it demands our admiring attention. At Ninfa the visitor seems to be stepping into a picture that has always been there in our dreams, but which we never imagined could be realized; the experience seems almost too good to be true.

Then again in both gardens the attention to detail is as wonderful as the larger pictures the visitor is offered: the Crane and the Carp, both symbols of long life, picked out in the pebble paving in Suzhou; the scarlet rose growing through the variegated maple at Ninfa. And because the details are so good we are required to move slowly, which adds to the sense of pensive appreciation. In both gardens all our senses are stimulated: we have already talked of the sounds of water at Ninfa, but there are also the smells trapped in the naves of ruined churches and the pleasures of walking over soft turf, which is redolent of the pastoral idyll, a common theme in so much European literature and painting. In the Wang Xi Yuan the pictures are miniatures, often framed in unpredictably shaped openings in the wall; sometimes they consist simply of the shadow of a tree or waving bamboo cast on a cream-coloured wall, which has been left deliberately unclothed by any climbing plants. Then the name of a pavilion invites us to concentrate on one sense impression or another; or maybe calls on us to meditate, for example, the Hall of the Accumulated Void. In both gardens what we might call the hard landscaping plays off against the softness of the planting, though in the Chinese garden the plants are scarcer. The advantage of this scarcity is that we look at each individual plant more intently; noting, for instance, the care with which an ancient wisteria has its twisting trunk supported

A moon gate frames an ornamental rock pile

on an equally aged crutch, we are reminded of the reverence with which the elderly are traditionally treated in Chinese culture.

But in the end the greatness of these gardens, and their way of lodging themselves in the memory, lies not in their appeal to the senses, nor in the rapt attention they solicit, nor in the intense, almost spiritual, calm they induce in the visitor; it also lies in their appeal to the intellect, the imagination, in the intensity of the experience they offer. At Ninfa the ruins of the medieval town in which the garden is made arouse half-shaped thoughts of *sic transit gloria mundi*, while also stimulating us to imagine what the buildings might once have looked like and how the ruined town might once have been peopled. In the Wang Xi the rock piles represent mountains in miniature, mountains which were the abode of the sages and the gods; a walk up and among these rocks, rather than along the easier, flat, pebbled paths of the main garden, stimulates thoughts of escape from the mundane world, thoughts of meditation and spiritual uplift. Thus the impressions these gardens make are, in a sense, endless; we never feel we have captured either garden whole, since there seems always so much more to think about, and even a second or third visit will not ensure that we feel we have got to the bottom of the experience in all its complexity. Afterwards, when we remember visits to these gardens, we will have a firm conviction that we have enjoyed a remarkable experience, but the plan of the garden's layout may not have lodged in our heads. There remains a mystery about these places, which is another reason they are unforgettable.

When we think of these two great gardens and what they have to offer, we must wonder if beauty is really the highest good that a garden can offer. The appeal to the intellect, to the imagination, and the atmosphere of the place are surely of greater value. Louisa Jones in her stimulating book *The Garden Visitor's Companion* recalls asking three friends 'What do you look for when you first enter a new garden?' This may be a good question to begin with, but the experienced garden visitor knows that, while looking will be the inevitable first response of someone living in such a visual age as ours, when the eye has been satisfied there will be the information from the other senses to attend to; and beyond all these will be that impalpable something called the atmosphere of the place. It will be this certain 'something', instinctively apprehended, that will decide whether the garden remains in our memory or not. Often it will be very hard to put into words what the atmosphere of a place is, and even harder to explain what causes us to feel such a response. In spite of these difficulties, David E. Cooper makes claims for the 'primacy' of atmosphere in shaping our response to the details of a garden: 'It is not simply that the explicit acts of perception come after the initial experience of atmosphere. In addition, they are crucially shaped and guided by it. This or that object of a subsequent perceptual act "stands out" or "emerges" as an appropriate object of explicit attention only in the context of the whole "setting".' The atmosphere provides what Cooper calls the setting, and it thus influences all the separate experiences we have in the garden; we notice individual details, in part, because of the atmosphere. For example, if a garden strikes us as 'spooky', we will pick up the details that reinforce and explain this reaction; thus at Hawkstone the eerie narrowness of the path between the damp, mossy rocks prepares our mood to appreciate other 'horrid' episodes in the garden.

And in gardens our senses are more alert than in an environment more completely subject to human control; like animals we pick up on signs that tell us what is going on in this place that is constantly changing. We are vulnerable in gardens because so much that can happen there is not only beyond our control but beyond our understanding. When we enter a garden we enter a world where many different kinds of living thing are going about their lives with a great sense of purpose, and this makes for a certain kind of unpredictability in the garden experience which requires us to be alert. As David E. Cooper puts it, 'because of this effortless alertness to the contingencies and novelties that affect us when in a garden, we become . . . "mindful", as Buddhists put it, not only of what is around us, but of our own physical engagement with it.' And just as a human reacts in a primitive, animal way to a felt, imminent danger, although the source of the danger cannot be seen, so in a garden we need all our senses, not just our eyes, to pick up the signals provided by the atmosphere of this strange, unpredictable place. Gardens constantly surprise us, so keep your eyes open, but all your other senses as well.

Occasionally it will be possible to offer some kind of rational account of why the garden seems replete with the atmosphere the visitor experiences. Russell Page, who created gardens full of rational, geometric lines and symmetry, responded, in particular, to the power of running water. In *The Education of a Gardener* he writes: 'If water is a necessity for the cultivation of plants it has other and less easily described functions. "White" water, breaking waves, waterfalls, cascades and fountain jets are known to produce negative ions, which "clear the air" and make people feel well. At the thirteenth-century Fountains Abbey in Yorkshire, the sick-bay was built over a weir on the river which flows under the buildings.' He goes on to describe visiting a garden that had 'a particularly agreeable and harmonious atmosphere', which at first he could not account for; only later did he discover that there were channels of water flowing under the flagstone paths.

The Islamic world has always understood the power of water over the mood of the garden visitor, and nowhere is this seen more clearly than in Iran. An outstanding example is the courtyard garden of the mausoleum of the Sufi holy man Shah Ne'mattolah Vali in Mahan. Here, the shallow, still, peat-dark pools reflecting towering, ancient cypresses as well as surrounding domes and minarets contribute significantly to the overwhelming sense of peace that makes this garden so memorable. All garden visitors must feel at some primitive, pre-verbal level of their being the exhilarating power of moving water and the calming effect of a still pool.

Light, too, can have a profound affect on the atmosphere of a place, sometimes by changing its apparent shape. The evening sun probing under trees will light up parts of the garden never seen at other times of the day, so that even those who have visited the garden frequently will be surprised. Equally powerful are the long shadows that may mysteriously conceal some important feature of the garden, or stimulate the imagination. The dawn sun can also throw the spotlight on to unexpected plants or a neglected piece of garden sculpture. The lingering dusk of summers in the more northerly latitudes can be a magic time, as the dew begins to rise and colours dim into each other, so that shapes become more prominent, if, eventually, indistinct. The mystery of a garden's layout may become more striking as darkness gathers. Smells, too, are powerful creators of atmosphere: the smell of roses in full bloom contained in a walled garden where the heat of the walls draws every last drop of scent from the flowers, or the drugged scent of newly mown grass, or a garden freshly watered after a long day of heat.

The Shrine of Ne'mattolah Vali, Mahan, Iran

In an interesting essay entitled 'Psychotopia' Tim Richardson explores the interaction of place (*topos*) with the human mind (*psyche*). He writes:

> Psychotopia is place understood not just in terms of location, but also in terms of meaning – its history, use, ecology, appearance, status, reputation, the people who interact with the place, its potential future. It refers to the actual life of the place as those who visit it experienced it, and therefore also encapsulates the psychic impact and accumulation of human consciousnesses. It does not only describe the atmosphere of a place as apprehended by the human mind . . . psychotopia addresses the dynamic manner in which the atmosphere works on us and, more controversially, how, in turn, our minds and experiences act on and influence places.

He argues that the visitor to a garden is always a co-creator (as is the case, surely, when we interact with music, painting, sculpture, poetry or any other of the arts), and that 'every time we experience a garden we remake it'. But he goes a step too far, as I see it, in arguing that places have minds and that they accumulate atmosphere from the impressions made on previous visitors.

All garden visitors will also be aware that there are certain elements in a garden that will militate against the creation of any kind of atmosphere. Too emphatic a statement of the garden's meaning, and an insistence on that meaning, as in many conceptualist gardens, will work against the numinous thing we call atmosphere. Massed bright colours, thumping you in the eye, will destroy the special sense of place by appealing too much to one sense alone, and will do nothing to draw the visitor's imagination into the process of experiencing the garden. The extraordinary Butchart Gardens on Vancouver Island provide an excellent example of a garden that has little charm because it is too colourful, too much aimed at delighting the eye alone. Then intrusive, loud noises from beyond the boundaries of the garden, such as the roar of aircraft taking off or of heavy traffic on a motorway, will destroy the concentration of the visitor and thus the atmosphere of the garden. The same will occur if there is too much talk among the visitors, distracting attention from what you have come to experience. Who would think of talking when seeing, for example, the Taj Mahal for the first time? Finally, sometimes if a garden is too tidy, too trim, it expresses a nervous tension that is destructive of atmosphere, like a house that is too tidy or a body too tightly corseted, and the hand of the human shaper is too obviously visible. The visitor must be able to relax into a dialogue with nature if the atmosphere is to do its work.

Some public gardens lack atmosphere because they lack personality; they seem designed and planted by a committee, not by an individual. And often in seeking to please all, they please none. An interesting case is a garden that has been private but has become public, perhaps after the death of the owner. The garden of La Landriana, 30 miles/50 kilometres south of Rome, was made in the post-war years by the Marchesa Lavinia Taverna and her husband; their first job was to clear the land of the explosives that the Allied advance on Rome had left behind. In her lifetime the garden was full of subtle plantings, contained in the firm structure that Russell Page had helped to give it. The Marchesa had her own ideas of how the garden should develop, and she did not always agree with Page, but their disagreements were productive and the result was a garden full of personality. Since her death, however, the property has been run by a foundation, and that has altered everything for the worse. When something dies, a plant is

The Butchart Gardens, Vancouver Island, Canada

now shoved in to take its place, and any plant, often the overflow from another part of the garden, so that the individual character of the different garden spaces has become blurred. And the maintenance of the garden is not as careful as it used to be. This can rarely be said of the National Trust gardens in England; they are looked after with great attention to detail, although they are sometimes too tidy, too neurotically perfect in their maintenance. But the organization tries to maintain the character and atmosphere of the individual gardens, rather than imposing the corporate uniformity that the visitor finds in the National Trust shops. The problem for such an organization is that it is looking after gardens that are monuments to particular periods or to remarkable individuals, and, if they are to do their memorializing work, such gardens must be conserved as they are. This means that they must not change, and to deny a garden the possibility of change or development is to deny it an essential part of its nature.

Ancient gardens, like many of those in the care of the National Trust, often seem imbued with a powerful atmosphere, largely because they readily work on our imaginations, but a garden need not be historic to have a strong atmosphere. The contemporary Parc André Citroen in Paris, created by Gilles Clément and Alain Provost, breathes an atmosphere of joy and celebration, yet is full of modern materials and its design is dominated by the clean geometry of straight lines. The two great greenhouses, for example, are rigidly rectangular with suspended glass walls, and the huge green space that lies at the heart of the garden is also perfectly rectangular. The fountains dance and sparkle, but they emerge from concrete paving slabs. This park not only pleases the eye but also remembers the importance of the other senses; the Jardins Serieles are six gardens devoted to the five corporeal senses and, interestingly, to a sixth sense, intuition. The atmosphere of some of the smaller spaces is controlled by colour; for example, the Black Garden is for calm, solitary activities, while the White Garden invites the visitor to be more lively and sociable. Here is a garden that does many of the things that all good gardens do – it stimulates us to think, to wonder, to admire, to respond, to imagine, to breathe deeply – but the components of the place that give rise to these experiences are interpreted and handled in a very modern style.

Can a formal garden with its quickly read layout ever have atmosphere? The garden at the Villa Lante, which has made so many appearances in this book, provides the answer. Yes, the design is as symmetrical as the most classical artist could wish; on the lowest level the twin pavilions echo each other as they preside

over the flat parterre with its low patterned hedges laid out, symmetrically, around the central fountain. What could be more obvious? More predictable? But all is not revealed at once; we look up the slope to the top of the first flight of steps and see there is much more to come. First there is the contrast of light and shade; the lowest parterre is full of sunlight, while above us the ancient plane trees with their mottled trunks cast deep shadows. Then we hear the sound of running water, inviting us to explore.

If, as T.S. Eliot wrote, 'Human kind cannot bear very much reality', then gardens may provide places of escape from a grindingly harsh real world. Even the Italian Renaissance princes of the Church needed an escape from the rituals of their small courts when they became too tediously demanding; they needed places to be private. At the Villa Farnese in Caprarola, for example, Cardinal Farnese would entertain state visitors in the palace he had had built on the foundations of a pentagonal castle, but further up the hill he could escape to the Casino del Piacere, a smaller building and an enclosed garden suited to more intimate pleasures. Like a good novel, gardens with a powerful atmosphere will transport us into another world, though this new horticultural world is harder to 'read' and harder to explain than the world of most fictions.

Opposite and above Parc André Citroen, Paris, France

Thus we say of some gardens, as of some novels and poems, that they are 'romantic'. What does it mean to call a garden 'romantic'? Perhaps that it appeals more to the imagination than to the intellect, because it is not ordered in a way that can easily and immediately be 'read'. And that its atmosphere, often compounded of mystery and beauty, is more important than its botanical collection, so romantic gardens never label their plants. Above all, it means a garden that seems to have been found rather than made, where the hand of the creator is concealed so that the garden seems to have happened without human intervention; the visitor seems to have stumbled upon it by happy chance. Untidiness will often be a mark of the romantic garden, but not too much untidiness or there will be no garden. Gardens neglected are often romantic. Who can forget the discovery Mary Lennox makes when she pushes open the door of the walled garden at her uncle's house in *The Secret Garden*? This garden had been neglected for ten years, yet it has some kind of magical power, healing Mary's cousin and, perhaps, making Mary a less unhappy, less cantankerous small girl.

Romantic gardens are often enclosed, either by thick vegetation or by walls, like Mary Lennox's secret garden; they are thus removed from the quotidian world and this makes them more appealing to the imagination. Also enclosed gardens store scents with great efficiency, and romantic gardens make a huge appeal to senses other than the eye. In Thomas Hardy's novel *Tess of the d'Urbervilles* the garden through which Tess passes, entranced as she listens to music played by Angel Clare, had been 'left uncultivated for several years'. Hardy gives us a wonderful description of the sensuous, even sensual, appeal of such a garden:

> Tall blooming weeds emitting offensive smells – weeds whose red and yellow and purple hues formed a polychrome as dazzling as that of cultivated flowers. She went stealthily as a cat through this profusion of growth, gathering cuckoo-spittle on her skirts, cracking snails that were underfoot, staining her hands with thistle-milk and slug-slime, and rubbing off upon her naked arms sticky blights which, though snow-white on the apple-tree trunks, made madder stains upon her skin.

Of all the senses only taste is not appealed to in this rich description of a romantic garden that helps the reader to appreciate Tess's experience of falling in love.

As Bacon memorably wrote, 'The breath of flowers is far sweeter in the air (where it comes and goes, like the warbling of musick) than in the hand,' and the scents trapped in the garden are always great triggers of memory; bypassing the intellect, they conjure up before us a scene we may imagine we have forgotten. Tim Richardson, expert on the most modern garden styles, has written that gardens 'are for many of us the most special places of all, filled with myriad threads of experience, emotion and memory which combine to make them meaningful'. This is particularly true of romantic gardens, though the garden's meaning is suggested rather than expounded. And gardens in ruins make the strongest appeal to the imagination. Complete, substantial buildings can impose themselves on a garden, while ruins seem to be deliquescing back to a natural state, and so more easily take their place in a garden composition. Ruins lead the mind back to the past, but to a past that is often romantically vague and thus the realm of dreams and speculation. Not all eighteenth-century British landscapers had the good fortune of the Aislabies at Studley Royal in north Yorkshire, who could include the ruins of Fountains Abbey in their composition. But ruins could be constructed, so that the newly moneyed owner of a great estate could suggest that his acres were part of an ancient heritage. Ruins continue to hold

Hidcote Manor, Chipping Campden, England

great fascination for garden makers; witness the recent importation to the Chelsea showground of the ruined glasshouse from Donhead Hall in Dorset. When asked what was the appeal of this decayed Victorian glasshouse, Stephen Woodhams, the designer of the show garden, replied: 'It was a magical moment to see how nature had overtaken the manmade.'

Can the design of a garden contribute to its romance and atmosphere? Certainly it can help to stimulate the imagination. The design can contribute to the atmosphere by creating mystery, not revealing all the garden at once; paths disappearing around corners, glimpses of what is to come through hedges, windows in walls – all these add to the sense of mystery. It is hard to imagine a garden that can be taken in at a glance having much atmosphere. Then there is the mystery of the empty, open space, not too large, and enclosed. At Castle Drogo in Devon Lutyens created a circular lawn surrounded by tall yew hedges, a strange, haunting, empty place, made more impressive by the contrast between this vacancy and the luxurious planting elsewhere in the garden. We are challenged to imagine what might take place in this empty circle; it seems created for ritual of some kind. On two recent visits to places created by friends, I have noticed circular spaces surrounded by trees, much less kempt than the Castle Drogo circle; the shapes are too perfect to have occurred naturally, so what can they be for? Might each be a threshing floor, a dance floor or a place for some kind of strange, secret ceremony? It might be a stage: we remember Peter Brook's line 'I can take any empty space and call it a bare stage. A man walks across this empty space while someone else is watching, and this is all that is needed for an act of theatre.' Later in the same work he claims 'the stage is a place where the invisible can appear', so if we wait long enough this empty garden circle may become populated by creatures of the place or of our imagination. One of the two circles has a bench at one side, which suggests that sometimes there are witnesses or an audience to see what is going on there. Or, perhaps, we the visitors are being asked to sit and meditate for a moment.

Gardens continue to fascinate us partly because, as John Dixon Hunt has written, 'The garden is a paradox, combining mathematics and magic, history and myth, science and art, reality and utopia.' He might have added individual personality and tradition, care and indifference, nature and human endeavour. Walter Pater in *Appreciations* claims that the function of art is 'not to teach lessons, or enforce rules, or even to stimulate to noble ends: but to withdraw the thoughts for a little while from the mere machinery of life, to fix them, with appropriate emotions, on the spectacle of those great facts in man's existence which no machinery effects'. In conveying meanings that lie beyond words, in taking us back to a pre-scientific appreciation of what is to be revered in nature, in enveloping the visitor in an unworldly atmosphere that is half dream while also acutely conscious of the power of time, the best gardens become magical places that lodge themselves deeply in the visitor's memory. Ludwig Wittgenstein wrote, 'Whereof one cannot speak, thereof one must be silent', but in one's silence it is possible to make a garden, which can speak for us.

Fountains Abbey, Ripon, England

8 THE WORLD'S TEN BEST GARDENS AND GARDEN EXPERIENCES

THE WORLD'S TEN BEST GARDENS

The order of these is not significant; nor is it intended that this list should be prescriptive – it rather aims to provoke debate. The list is, of course, the result of one man's taste, no more; however, it is a taste informed by years of looking at gardens in many parts of the world with an increasingly critical eye – an eye, I hope, in Hume's words, 'improved by practice, perfected by comparison and cleared of all prejudice'. Necessarily the list is provisional – the next garden one visits may challenge those already in the top ten, or provide a unique garden experience. In my notes on this top ten I have tried to bear in mind the five requirements of good criticism discussed earlier – that it should describe, classify, contextualize, interpret and, finally, evaluate.

Wang Shi Yuan, Suzhou, China

This is a classic, Chinese scholar's garden in the town of Suzhou, about 100 miles/ 160 kilometres west of Shanghai. It is a walled garden packed with incident and interest, all fitted into a site that is little more than an acre/0.4 hectares. But the garden is laid out with such a subtle sense of the dramatic that we are constantly led on to explore, and as constantly taken by surprise, so that we quickly become disorientated, with the result that this small garden seems vast. Every view has been carefully planned, and no detail been neglected, down to the designs in the pebble paving. There is a total absence of symmetry, which at first disconcerts the Western visitor, until we realize that symmetry, in the Oriental mind, occurs only in what is dead; it is too balanced, too still. There are few plants in the Wang Xi Yuan, though each is perfectly sited, sometimes to throw shadows on to the wall of the garden, or placed in isolation so that we can appreciate its twisting form, brimming with the energy of 'ch'i'. The twisted, contorted shapes of the Taihu rocks emit the same

sense of energy barely contained; their pitted surfaces show the complementary 'yin' and 'yang' of solid contrasting with void. And the naming of the pavilions shows acute awareness of all the senses that may be stimulated in a garden: the Pavilion for Listening to the Wind in the Pine, for example. Since the rock piles are miniaturized mountains, and in Chinese tradition the mountains are the abode of sages and gods, ascending one of these rock piles by a set of winding, narrow steps (they are described in one Chinese garden manual as twisting like kittens at play) takes the visitor out of the mundane world and encourages a more elevated, spiritual state of mind – the function, perhaps, of every garden. The paths are narrow, and the bridges over the streams are zig-zagged, so it is impossible to hurry through the garden; we have to enjoy it slowly and pensively. As the Chinese-American writer Yi-Fu Tuan says in *Topophilia*, 'To walk in a Chinese garden and be aware of even a fraction of its total meaning is to enter a world that rewards the senses, the mind and the spirit.' It is this totality of experience, where head, heart and spirit are stimulated and satisfied, that makes the Wang Xi Yuan such a great garden. And when your visit is finished, it will be almost impossible to remember the plan of the garden; you have been lost in another world, like the fisherman in the story of Peach Blossom Spring (see page 101).

Hidcote Manor, Gloucestershire, England

This is the most influential twentieth-century garden in England, made by an American immigrant, Lawrence Johnston, who was the re-inventor and best exponent of the idea of garden rooms. This was not just an aesthetic decision: he had to plant hedges to protect his plants from the winds that whistle along the edge of the Cotswold escarpment where the garden is situated. The hedges themselves are interesting for the variety of textures achieved by mixing the plants that compose them – holly, yew and beech, both green and purple. But some visitors feel the hedges are too high and the spaces they enclose too small, even claustrophobic; I suspect this says something about Johnston's shy character. Again there are constant surprises and variety, of colours, of proportions, of views opening and closing, such as the long view down the green walk to the countryside, and the view from the edge of the Cotswold escarpment. This spaciousness contrasts with, for example, the raised circular swimming pool jammed into a space that is much too small for it, and the garden rooms in which the detailed planting is exquisitely planned, but sometimes almost too intense. The White Garden and the Red Border are subtly organized, although the plantings are no longer Johnston's, and they contrast with the spaces that are all green, such as the Theatre Lawn and the Stilt Garden. The final surprise is the Stream Garden, where all is curved and relaxed, though the planting is still abundant. Johnston was a plantsman and a plant collector, but at Hidcote he demonstrates how a fascination with individual plants can go hand in hand with artistry in their use, and how the tight control exercised by architectural planting can harmonize with an exuberant use of flowers.

The garden of the Nezu Museum (formerly the Nezu Institute of Fine Arts), Tokyo, Japan

The 5-acre/2-hectare garden lies in a valley behind the former home of Nezu Kaichiro (1860–1940), a railway magnate who left his art collection to the nation. The garden contains several tea houses, since Kaichiro was a follower of the 'way of tea', and the utensils of the tea ceremony are a major feature of the museum's collection. It is such a relief to escape from the hideous architecture of this rampantly consumerist city into the calm beauty of the Nezu garden. The steeply sloping sides of the valley give you the feeling of being quite isolated from the world. And this is a Japanese garden to be explored, not merely looked at from a fixed point of view, a kind of modern 'stroll' garden; the twisting paths and curved lines of stepping stones ensure that the visitor moves slowly, as is essential if we are to appreciate every tiny, immaculate detail. It has many of the classic features of the Japanese garden, but is not so refined nor freighted with religious symbolism as many of the classic Kyoto gardens. Delightful small scenes constantly take away your breath, but the artistry is concealed in an apparently relaxed and informal layout. It is the ideal introduction to the careful attention to detail that is so satisfying in the Japanese garden – the bamboo fences held together by cord that is elegantly knotted, the rounded stepping stones laid in a beautiful curving pattern, the perfectly proportioned stone bridges. While in some Japanese gardens the shaping hand of the designer gives the whole composition a starchy perfection that can be almost repellent, because it militates against any imaginative appreciation of atmosphere, here the beauty of the man-made components of the garden scene do not seem at odds with the relaxed, natural growth of the plants.

Innisfree, Millbrook, New York, USA

This garden, or rather landscape, was made by Walter and Marion Beck between 1930 and 1960. Lester Collins, a landscape architect, then took on the development of the site until his death in 1993. The Becks had been influenced by Chinese scroll paintings of gardens, particularly that of the eighth-century poet Wang Wei. Thus the garden presents a sequence of pictures, and the whole garden can not be seen from any one point. Innisfree is an estate of 150 acres/60 hectares laid out around the stillness of a 40-acre/16-hectare glacial lake. It is a characteristically American garden, celebrating the wilderness, but influenced by the Chinese tradition, whose models have been reinterpreted in a local idiom. The garden is made from the components of the wilderness landscape – lakes, streams, trees, rocks and grass. These have been nudged into more satisfying shapes, but in such a way that the whole landscape seems almost natural; for example, the mossed stones standing beside the lake could have been left behind by glacial activity, but in fact they have been erected so that the 'yang' of the stone contrasts with and complements the 'yin' of the water. Most of the trees are indigenous to the site and most of the rocks were found near by. Only the water jets and the rock terraces could not be part of the natural landscape, but these are introduced so gently that the transition from natural to man-made is almost imperceptible. There is some small-scale, detailed gardening on the terraces, but it is so relaxed, with plants allowed to self-seed in the cracks of the paving, that it does not disturb the peaceful naturalness of the site. Most of the art is found in the shaping of the mounds and hills, the placing and arrangement of rocks, the grouping of trees and the contrived, extravagant meandering of a stream. Here is a celebration of the majesty and scale of the American wilderness, but subtly shaped and improved by the hand of man.

The Alhambra/Generalife complex, Granada, Spain

In the Alhambra the noble simplicity of the Court of the Myrtles takes away the breath. The central, rectangular pool is so much bigger than might be expected, and brings reflections and light into a space that might otherwise feel claustrophobic. The confident calm of the atmosphere must have impressed visiting ambassadors, who were received in a pavilion at one end of the courtyard, and thus perhaps contributed to the longevity of Granada's independence as an Islamic state; it only fell to the Christian powers in 1492. By contrast the Court of the Lions is exquisite, almost domestic in its proportions. Here water moves, improbably, from the buildings towards the central fountain, sparkling in the sunlight. And the whole scene can be enjoyed from the shade of the colonnade that runs on elegantly etiolated pillars around the central space. In neither of these courtyards are plants of the highest importance; in the Court of the Myrtles there are only severely pruned myrtle hedges, and in the Court of the Lions there are now no plants, though once there would have been some, perhaps fruit trees, in sunken beds, below the level of the paving. The drama and simplicity of these garden spaces is remarkable. Water gives movement, variety and sound, while the light and shadows as they move also add to the complexity of the garden experience. The beauty of proportion, so often a major attraction in an Islamic garden, can here be appreciated to the full.

After the austerity of the Alhambra, the plant-filled grounds of the Generalife still have the feeling that they are pleasure gardens – indulgent, glamorous and sensual. Here there is more colour, and the water is used playfully, as in the famous Patio de la Acequia, where small fountains arch in pairs from each side of a long, rectangular canal. Further up the hillside water even runs merrily down the banister of a staircase. From the pavilions in the garden one can look out at the harsh surrounding landscape of scrawny trees and barren, yellow earth, and feel the sense of privilege and relief that those in paradise must feel when looking down on those in hell!

Lotusland, California, USA

This garden is certainly way out, and way over the top, but it is so unusual and personal that it is unmissable. Lotusland was created by an unsuccessful singer, whose stage name was Ganna Walska, between 1941 and her death in 1984. Unsuccessful she may have been as a singer, but she was certainly successful in attracting wealthy men, five of whom she married. And she spent the proceeds from these marriages largely on this remarkable garden. The lady's taste is everywhere to be seen, and even if it is not yours, you cannot fail to respond to the conviction and imagination with which it is expressed. It is claimed that she called herself 'the enemy of the average', and there is little of the 'average' about her garden. The use of cactus and euphorbia to line the main drive is intensely original, and at the front of the house these same plants have an extraordinary effect, some seeming like paint squeezed from a tube. Though the giant shells around the pool may have a feeling of Hollywood, compare this garden to that of Hearst Castle in California to see how much more style and character this has; the Hearst garden has only money. A Water Garden, a Japanese Garden (not very successful), a Tropical Garden and many other specialist gardens find room on this 35-acre/14-hectare estate. Perhaps most memorable is the Blue Garden, where *Cedrus atlantica* 'Glauca' lords it over blue fescue grass and the paths are lined with blue glass, the slag from a local bottle factory. Typical of the theatrical style of the whole place is the Topiary Garden, with a topiary clock 25 feet/8 metres in diameter. An additional pleasure is that the maintenance is of an unusually high standard, a necessary condition in such a highly artificial garden.

Villa Lante, Bagnaia, Italy

This is a late sixteenth-century classic Italian garden, probably designed by Vignola for Cardinal Gambara, Bishop of Viterbo. It is not a grand garden and all the more appealing for that. Its setting – in a park, rather than near a house – makes it feel more of a retreat than a space for exhibition; many Italian gardens, taking their cue from Bramante's Belvedere courtyard, seem like stages where the owner and friends could parade, very conscious of making *la bella figura*. This garden is a long, rectangular, walled strip that runs down the hillside in a series of terraces, shaded by ancient plane trees. Each terrace is treated differently, and at the bottom sunlight fills a rectangular parterre. The playful use of abundant water, unforgettably flowing at one point down the middle of a stone dining table, gives a lightness and movement to the whole experience. And the contrast between light and shade, so central to any Italian garden's success, is here beautifully controlled. The garden's programme (see Chapter 6) may now be obscure, but there is no missing the coat of arms of its creator, the crayfish (*gambero*) of Gambara. For all that he was a cardinal and the bishop, it is impossible to find any Christian emblem in the garden; the references are all to the world of classical myth. Perhaps he was too worldly; certainly church reformers admonished him for spending too much money merely for pleasure, when he should have been giving more to help the poor and needy. The garden has been hardly changed since its creation. In 1590 the Montalto family took it over; they built the second summer house, which had always been planned as the twin to that built by Gambara, and added the statues of the four handsome youths bearing their family's emblem which now stands at the centre of the fountain on the flat parterre, but otherwise they made no important changes.

Mount Stewart, Newtownards, Northern Ireland

There are many things wrong with the UK's National Trust, but their care of this 1920s garden, created by Edith, Marchioness of Londonderry, with some assistance from Lutyens and Jekyll, cannot be faulted. To see immaculate, high-input gardening, this is the place to come. The garden itself is not only beautifully planted and beautifully planned but full of idiosyncrasies, such as the Dodo Terrace, where grotesque stone animals represent some of the Londonderrys' closest friends, including Winston Churchill. Because it lies on the east shore of Strangford Lough temperatures never fall very low, so that a surprisingly wide range of plants can be grown. Thus in the Mairi Garden (named after Lady Londonderry's youngest daughter), where the dominant colours are blue and white, we find many plants from Australia and New Zealand. Then there is an Italian garden, with details borrowed from the Palazzo Farnese at Caprarola and the Villa Gamberaia, a blue and white garden, a Spanish garden and, coming closer to home, both a shamrock garden and a garden displaying the red hand of Ulster. Across the lake the visitor looks up to a hill where the family are buried, called Tir na n'Og (the Land of the Eternally Young). The Moghul emperors, too, were buried in gardens; they are good places for memory and reflection, and their beauty consoles the mourners who are left behind. This is a public garden that has preserved much of the atmosphere of its days as a private pleasure ground, and the personality of its creator is still strongly felt.

The Majorelle Garden, Marrakech, Morocco

This again is a town garden cut off from its urban surroundings by walls. It is a rare garden because the colour green is far from dominant; the colour that strikes the visitor and that we remember is the deep, ultramarine blue that has come to be known as Majorelle blue, a colour surely influenced by the colour of Berber robes. The outside of the house is painted in this colour, as are many of the flower pots; others are painted an equally unexpected, intense canary yellow. The paths in this extraordinary garden are the colour of brick. The influence of the Islamic tradition is felt in the use of moving water – the pools, the rills and the fountains. Contrasting with this is the use of desert plants, mainly cactuses and succulents, with height provided by coconut palms and banana trees. This is a painter's garden, created in the 1920s by Jacques Majorelle when he left France for health reasons. After his death the garden was neglected, until taken in hand by Yves Saint Laurent and Pierre Bergé. The garden was reproduced in part at the 1997 Chelsea Flower Show and had an immediate effect in English gardens – deep blue flower pots were to be seen throughout the land. After experiencing this garden, an Italian visitor described it as 'a monument to the beauty of life, and to the joy of living'. Any garden that has such an effect on a visitor must be a success.

Seeing dawn rise in the garden of the Taj Mahal, Agra, India

You watch the light change on the Taj Mahal's beautiful dome from pearl grey at the first hint of dawn, to flamingo pink, to ivory white, with infinite gradations of shading in between. The garden's shapes are first defined in black and white, the heavy accents being the evergreens. As the light brightens tones become clearer, and finally colours emerge. Then the fountains begin to play and refract the beams of sunlight, so that the whole place comes magically to life.

Entering the Green Garden at Knightshayes, near Tiverton, Devon, England

The great moment here at this garden, remade in the 1950s by Sir John and Lady Amory, begins when you find yourself standing in front of the low, multi-coloured, flat garden near the house; to the right there is an opening in a tall, yew hedge. Thus you enter one of the most magical garden spaces, which contrasts completely with the lively, low colours outside. If you are not prepared for it, the moment will take your breath away. This beautifully proportioned, hedged, green garden contains an oval pool, a silver pear tree, a statue and a stone bench – that's all. As so often in great works of art, less is more.

Going on a bright sunny day to Snowshill Manor in the Cotswold Hills, to enjoy a remarkable sequence of light and shade

You move from the lowest, enclosed garden, filled with sunlight, through the dark barn, and then the copse, and up the steps to gasp at the view that suddenly and unexpectedly opens up to your left. The drama of light and shade strikes you as soon as you leave the sun-filled garden, stuffed with plants in raised beds, and enter the gloom of the barn. From the back there is a path through a copse of *Viburnum opulus*, dappled with sunlight. Finally, after the experience of shade, you climb the steps at the end of this woodland path, and the light is overwhelming, as is the excitement of the sweeping view to the left, down and out over the sunlit Cotswold sheep pasture. Light and shade, enclosure and openness – great garden experiences are often built of contrasts.

Glimpsing, at Branitz in Germany, the reflection of the island pyramid where Prince Hermann Puckler Pückler-Muskau is at rest, beside his long-suffering wife, Lucie

On the grave is this inscription: 'Gravestones are the mountain tops of a distant, lovely land'. Pückler-Muskau was an obsessive, insatiable maker of parks, saying that anyone who wanted to know him must begin by examining his parks, 'for my park is my heart'. He certainly sacrificed everything and everyone to this obsession. He was constantly running out of money, both his own and his wife's. And it was this lack of funds that took him to England in an endeavour to trade the title of Princess for a fortune. He failed to find an heiress, and therefore had to sell his original estate at Muskau and move to this smaller park, which he set about remaking with undimmed enthusiasm. In some ways a monster, as a park maker he was heroic.

Reflecting at Vaux le Vicomte, near Paris, France, on how the display of wealth (a temptation for so many garden makers) can lead to a fall

This extraordinary garden 35 miles/56km south-east of Paris was created in the mid-seventeenth century by Nicolas Fouquet, Louis XIV's finance minister. Regardless of expense, Fouquet employed the most eminent artists of the day on both the chateau and the garden; Louis le Vaux was his architect, Charles le Brun his designer and painter, and André le Nôtre his garden maker. In 1661 the conclusion of work on the garden was celebrated with a lavish reception to which Fouquet invited the King. This was a mistake. The King, perhaps not a little jealous, inquired where all the money had come from to pay for such an impressive garden. Fouquet was arrested and spent the rest of his life in prison, while Louis took le Nôtre and many of the statues and trees off to embellish his own great creation, Versailles. Gardens can reveal too much of their makers.

Emerging from a labyrinth of narrow, dark passageways into the light and the elegantly proportioned space of the Courtyard of the Myrtles at the Alhambra, Granada, Spain

There is almost nothing there – which shows again how dramatic empty space can be. The only plants are the myrtle hedges, though once there were orange trees in pots; the only colour is their green and some Azulejos tiles on the end wall. The whole space is dominated by the stillness of the central, dark, rectangular pool, though small, low fountains bubble up from pavement level. As so often in Islamic gardens the proportions of the courtyard are perfectly conceived and are a major component of its beauty. The stillness and confidence of this space must have conveyed a political message to those who visited this small Muslim state from the Christian north of Spain.

Discovering William Martin's contemporary garden at Wigandia, Noorat, Australia, atop an extinct volcano

Many Australian gardens are pale, sickly imitations of European models; particularly common are rose gardens full of disease and ungainly plants. The other thing widely on offer is a garden featuring a collection of native Australian plants, all whippy, stringy, wiry things. But Martin's garden is different; he embraces the conditions instead of seeming to resent them. Patterns of plump, grey-leaved echeverias and other succulents are planted directly into the brick-coloured volcanic ash, and the sculpture is all rusty-iron farm implements.

The garden is a work of defiant genius, which Martin calls 'my private adventure ground'. His stubborn originality is typified in an article he wrote titled 'The Importance of Not Gardening'; one of the things saved by following his advice is water.

Gasping at the view from the terrace at the Villa Cimbrone, Ravello, Italy
If you approach this in the right way (by keeping in the shade and to the right through the garden), nothing will prepare you for this spectacular view. I will say nothing more. The garden in some ways is typically Edwardian English, but its position was described by the nineteenth-century German traveller Gregorovius as 'incomparable'.

Escaping at the Palazzo Farnese in Caprarola, Italy, from the rectangular formality of the Winter and Summer Gardens under the walls of the palazzo into the woodland

Through a gap in the trees, you suddenly glimpse, hovering above the glittering spray of the fountains, a supremely elegant loggia, quite small in comparison to the majestic bulk of the palazzo itself (it had been a pentagonal fortress before Vignola got to work on it). It is quite unexpected, a magical place surrounded by trees and quite cut off from the world. This is the Casino del Piacere (the Pleasure Pavilion), to which the Cardinal could retire when fed up with the pomp and politics of his miniature court. Here he could escape not only the burden of state affairs but also the formal behaviour expected of him in the palazzo. The enclosed garden on one side of the Casino provides the ideal setting for such an escape – and escape is part of what gardens are all about.

Enjoying Burle Marx's work in and near Rio de Janeiro, Brazil

The inventiveness of the man is seen in the garden he created beside the Centro Empresarial, a giant of a skyscraper. What could he do in such a narrow site, so dominated by a concrete monster? He decided, remarkably, to sink the garden and design it in elaborate detail, which draws the eye downward. Then he marked it with a line of stately royal palms, which grow tall to give some shade, their slender elegance contrasting with the weight of the concrete that hangs over them. Then the wit of the man: the seat he designed for the Largo do Machado is a immensely long, free-flowing snake of a concrete bench which makes one smile, but is also practical since it cannot easily be vandalized and, as it writhes in and out of the sun, the sitter can chose cool or heat. The paving schemes he designed for public areas, in Chaim Weitzman Square, for example, or at the Caemi Foundation, or, most famously, along the seafront at Copacabana, take free modern forms. Similar shapes are found in the abstract tapestries that can be seen at the house, the Sìtio, where this protean genius lived – musician, sculptor, painter, weaver, gardener, botanist, potter.

SELECT BIBLIOGRAPHY

Elizabeth von Arnim, *Elizabeth and Her German Garden* (1898)

Diana Athill, *Somewhere Towards the End* (Granta, 2008)

W.H. Auden, *The Dyer's Hand* (Faber, 1962)

Peter Brook, *The Empty Space* (MacGibbon and Kee, 1968)

Karel Capek, *The Gardener's Year* (translated by M. and R. Weatherall), (George, Allen and Unwin, 1931)

Noël Carroll, *On Criticism* (Routledge, 2009)

Beth Chatto and Christopher Lloyd, *Dear Friend and Gardener* (Frances Lincoln, 1998)

David E. Cooper, *A Philosophy of Gardens* (Oxford, 2006)

Freda Cox, *Garden Styles* (Crowood Press, 2010)

Sheppard Craige, *Words in the Woods* and *Il Bosco della Ragnaia* (Edizioni della Ragnaia, 2004 and 2007)

Paula Deitz, *Of Gardens* (University of Philadelphia Press, 2011)

Mark Francis and Randolph T. Hester Jr. (eds), *The Meaning of Gardens* (M.I.T. Press, 1990)

Martin Hoyles, *Gardener's Delight* (Pluto Press, 1994)

John Dixon Hunt, Jeffrey Kipnis and Gavin Keeney, *On the Nature of Things* (Birkhauser Verlag, 2000)

Louisa Jones, *The Garden Visitor's Companion* (Thames and Hudson, 2009)

Patrick Lane, *What the Stones Remember* (Trumpeter Books, 2005)

Philip Larkin, *High Windows* (Faber and Faber, 1974)

William Morris, *Art and Social Reform* (London, 1882)

Rudolf Otto (translated by John W. Harvey), *The Idea of the Holy* (Penguin Books, 1959)

Russell Page, *The Education of a Gardener* (Penguin Books, 1985)

Thomas Pakenham, *Meetings with Remarkable Trees* (Cassell, 1997)

Tim Richardson, *Avant Gardeners* (Thames and Hudson, 2008)

Tim Richardson and Noël Kingsbury (eds.), *Vista* (Frances Lincoln, 2005): includes Tim Richardson's essay 'Psychotopia'

Philip Robinson (ed.), *The Faber Book of Gardens* (2007)

William Robinson, *The English Flower Garden* (8th edition, John Murray, 1900): contains a section on the use of colour in the flower border, written by Gertrude Jekyll

John D. Sedding, *Garden Craft Old and New* (Kegan, Paul 1891)

Graham Stuart Thomas, *The Art of Planting* (J.M. Dent. 1984)

David Wheeler (ed.), *Hortus Revisited* (Frances Lincoln, 2008)

Margaret Willes, *The Making of the English Gardener* (Yale, 2011)

Note: Page numbers in *italics* refer to captions to the illustrations

120
see also Austen, Jane;
   Bassani, Georgio; James,
   Henry
Little Sparta, Dunsyre,
   Scotland 30–31
Littlecote, Wiltshire 37
Lloyd, Christopher 38, 56
   use of colour 83–4, 85,
   87
Londonderry, Edith,
   Marchioness of 140
Lotusland, California 136,
   137
Louis XIV 17, 148
Luhan, Mabel 79
Lutyens, Edwin 122, 140

M
Majorelle, Jacques 142
Majorelle Garden,
   Marrakech 142, *143*
Mandela, Nelson 16
Mapperton, Dorset 96–7
Marchi, Marcello 77
Marcus, Clare Cooper 23
Martin, William 150
Marx, Roberto Burle 87,
   153, *153*
meaning and metaphor 23,
   98, 123
   eighteenth-century
   England 99–100
   Italian Renaissance
   gardens 98–9
   learning cultural
   interpretation 102–3
   oriental and Islamic
   gardens 100–101, 102,
   103–4

over-emphasized 116
   political 128, 149
   use of words 103–5
Mecca 22
memories
   childhood 11, 30, 108
   and experience 109–
   110, 112
   folk 108
   of other gardens 32
Miller, Arthur, *Death of a
   Salesman* 9
Miller, Mara 18
Mitford, Nancy 37
Monticello, Virginia, USA
   36
Morin, Pierre 34
Morris, William 83
Mount Stewart, Northern
   Ireland 140, *141*
Munstead Wood, Surrey
   47

N
National Gardens Scheme
   38–9, 41
National Trust gardens
   117, 140
Ne'mattolah Vali shrine,
   Mahan, Iran 114, *115*
Nezu Kaichiro 130
Nezu Museum garden,
   Tokyo 130, *131*
Ninfa, Lazio *109*, 110–12,
   128, *129*
Nonsuch, Surrey 34
Northumberland, Duchess
   of 64, 66
Nymens, Sussex 37

O
The Old Vicarage, East
   Ruston, Norfolk 58–
   64, *59*, *60*, *63*
Omar Khayyám 12
oriental gardens 17–18,
   33, 95–6
   see also Chinese gardens;
   Japanese gardens
Orsini, Pier Francesco 91
Osti, Gian Lupo 21
Otto, Rudolf 19
Oxford college gardens 30

P
Packenham, Thomas 21
Page, Russell 89, 90, 106–
   7, 114, 116
Parc André Citroen, Paris
   117–18, *119*
Parkinson, John 82
parterres 34, 79, 80
Pasternak, Boris 84
Pater, Walter 103, 122–3
paving patterns 52–3
Paxton, Joseph 93
Paysage, Nip 18
Persian gardens 95–6, 102
   Bagh-e Fin, Kashan 27,
   28
   Ne'mattolah Vali shrine
   114, *115*
Petrarch 15
photography 45, 98,
   109–10
place-making 13, 15, 22
plant collectors' gardens
   57, 126
Platter, Thomas 34
post-traumatic stress